cook's kitchen reference

MEAT

cook's kitchen reference

MEAT

all you need to know about choosing, preparing
and cooking meat, plus 50 delicious recipes

Lucy Knox and Keith Richmond

LORENZ BOOKS

This edition is published by Lorenz Books

Lorenz Books is an imprint of Anness Publishing Ltd
Hermes House, 88–89 Blackfriars Road, London SE1 8HA
tel. 020 7401 2077; fax 020 7633 9499
www.lorenzbooks.com; info@anness.com

© Anness Publishing Ltd 2001, 2006

UK agent: The Manning Partnership Ltd, 6 The Old Dairy, Melcombe Road, Bath BA2 3LR;
tel. 01225 478444; fax 01225 478440; sales@manning-partnership.co.uk

UK distributor: Grantham Book Services Ltd, Isaac Newton Way, Alma Park Industrial Estate, Grantham, Lincs NG31 9SD;
tel. 01476 541080; fax 01476 541061; orders@gbs.tbs-ltd.co.uk

North American agent/distributor: National Book Network, 4501 Forbes Boulevard, Suite 200, Lanham, MD 20706;
tel. 301 459 3366; fax 301 429 5746; www.nbnbooks.com

Australian agent/distributor: Pan Macmillan Australia, Level 18, St Martins Tower, 31 Market St, Sydney, NSW 2000;
tel. 1300 135 113; fax 1300 135 103; customer.service@macmillan.com.au

New Zealand agent/distributor: David Bateman Ltd, 30 Tarndale Grove, Off Bush Road, Albany, Auckland;
tel. (09) 415 7664; fax (09) 415 8892

A CIP catalogue record for this book is available from the British Library.
Publisher: Joanna Lorenz
Managing Editor: Linda Fraser
Senior Editor: Margaret Malone
Designer: Nigel Partridge
Photographers: Craig Robertson (recipe section) and Janine Hosegood
Stylist: Helen Trent
Food for Photography: Joanna Farrow and Bridget Sargeson, assisted by
Victoria Walters (recipe section); and Annabel Ford (reference section)

Previously published as *Cook's Guide to Meat*

1 3 5 7 9 10 8 6 4 2

NOTES

Bracketed terms are intended for American readers. Medium (US large) eggs are used
unless otherwise stated. For all recipes, quantities are given in both metric and imperial
measures and, where appropriate, measures are also given in standard cups and
spoons. Follow one set, but not a mixture, because they are not interchangeable.
Standard spoon and cup measures are level.
1 tsp = 5ml, 1 tbsp = 15ml, 1 cup = 250ml/8fl oz
Australian standard tablespoons are 20ml. Australian readers should use 3 tsp in place
of 1 tbsp for measuring small quantities of gelatine, flour, salt etc.

Contents

INTRODUCTION

Meat is probably our favourite food. In every meat-eating culture in the world, it is the food for a feast, a celebration or any special occasion. Every one of our festivals – Christmas and Easter in Britain, Thanksgiving and Mardi Gras in the United States, Hanukkah in the Jewish calendar, not to mention the many anniversaries and feast days – centres around a special meal, and in each one meat is almost always the central component.

However, meat is more than just a festive food. All those who enjoy meat do so because it not only tastes superb served in large joints, but also because it is delicious when cooked and served in more modest portions. Meat, above all, is versatile. It can be fried, grilled (broiled), poached or stewed, served with pasta, rice, grains or vegetables, or cooked with just about anything. There is really no limit to the ways that meat can be used.

The first domesticated animals

Meat has been eaten for as long as humans have been able to catch the animals. At first the animals were wild, but it wasn't long before ancient man began to domesticate animals such as cows, sheep and pigs. The animals were reared for their milk, skins and wool as well as for their meat or, in the case of buffalo and oxen, for their ability to pull the first ploughs and early carts.

Sheep were first domesticated by the tribes of Central Asia 10,000 years ago, and by 2000 BC, farmers in China, Egypt and the Middle and Near East had learned to domesticate cattle, pigs and sheep for their meat.

The historical importance of meat

Meat has played a central role in the development of agriculture, industry and commerce in almost every country in the world, and it is often referred to in historical texts. The Old Testament is full of references to eating meat, from Genesis onwards. In the New Testament, too, there are countless stories where meat symbolizes worship and celebration. When the Prodigal Son returns to his home, his father cries, "bring the fattened calf and kill it. Let's have a feast and celebrate."

Elsewhere in literature, whether calf, lamb or oxen, meat features regularly, symbolizing wealth, prosperity and good living. Conversely, poverty and need is regularly symbolized by a lack of meat at the table. People would calculate their position in society by how frequently meat was served. For the greater part of history in Britain and most parts of Europe, meat was a luxury food for all but the well off. Kings and queens may have dined on all sorts of wonderful roasts and meats, but for ordinary people, meat was eked out to add much sought-after flavour and

Above: Farmers have realized that well-cared for cows produce better meat.

protein to broths and stews that otherwise were made up of meal, and vegetables if they were lucky.

Until very recently, meat was far and away the most expensive component of a meal and, in times of shortages, it was inevitably the first ingredient on which to cut back. Throughout history, people have made the most of meat by serving it with economical starchy ingredients and accompaniments such as pastry, dumplings or Yorkshire puddings to make a little go a long way.

In fact, it is thanks entirely to the less affluent members of society that we have so many different recipes for cooking meat. Stews, casseroles, tagines, hot-pots, pies and cassoulets are among the hundreds of ways devised by ordinary people for using the poorer, less tender cuts of meat.

The influence of religion and custom

It is not only cost that determines how much meat is eaten; consumption also varies according to religion, custom and taste. Beef is one of the most popular meats in most countries, except in India where Hindus do not eat the flesh of the

Left: After years of being farmed intensively indoors, many pigs nowadays are being reared in the traditional ways and enjoying a far more pleasant life outdoors in the fresh air.

cow, which they consider to be sacred. Meanwhile Muslims and Jews will not eat pork or any meat that hasn't been killed in a specific ritual way. British people will not eat horsemeat or dogmeat, although the former is much enjoyed in the rest of Europe and the latter in much of the Far East.

Better farming

In most countries, there are no religious laws underpinning meat preparation, and consequently the meat available in our shops continues to change, as methods of breeding and butchery improve. Meat today is vastly superior in flavour and texture to that available even 20 years ago. Farmers have responded to concerns about healthy eating, and are breeding animals that provide leaner meat. In addition, they are realizing that the more care lavished on cows or pigs, the better the meat. Customers in turn are demanding this

too, both because of concern about the welfare of animals and because of a desire for good, lean meat.

There is no doubt that free-range pork tastes far better than the meat from pigs reared on factory-like farms. As a result, more and more farmers are reverting to traditional, often organic, methods where animals are allowed to graze freely outdoors, free from both chemicals and pesticides.

Organic and traditionally reared meat is becoming increasingly available from specialist butchers' and many larger supermarkets. It costs a little more than intensively reared meats, but is considered to be superior in every respect, being healthier, with better flavour and a leaner and more tender texture. Most of us are also considerably happier knowing that the meat we are cooking with and eating comes from an animal that was properly treated when alive.

Above: Sheep were the first animals to be domesticated and are now farmed all over the world often in small mountain flocks.

This is especially true of calves. Veal was considered a delicacy in Medieval Europe and has remained a popular premium meat ever since. In the 1990s, though, consumption of veal declined in Britain and North America because of concerns over the methods used in raising the animals. But a commitment by farmers to more humane farming methods has seen veal come back into fashion and nowadays a wide range of cuts are available from good butchers'.

Preserved and cured meats

Meat was once butchered at home and cut into convenient portions for eating there and then, or it was preserved by drying, salting or smoking for eating throughout the year. Nowadays of course, thanks to modern transportation and refrigeration, fresh and frozen meat is widely available throughout the year from butchers' and supermarkets. However, despite the availability of fresh meat, many of the cured meats such as bacon and ham, which our ancestors preserved out of necessity, are still produced and eaten today simply because they taste very good.

Other meat products, which were once made to preserve meat, include fresh, smoked and cured sausages. These were originally produced to use up the scraps of pork left after home-reared pigs had been butchered. They

Below: Although dried and cured meats are no longer produced out of necessity, they remain popular throughout the world. This butchers' shop in Normandy, France has a wide range of dried sausages and cured meats for sale along with various kinds of fresh meat.

Right: Buy from a traditional butcher who will offer a wide range of lovingly prepared small cuts and special joints.

are still made throughout the world but nowadays sausages are more likely to be produced in a factory than in the home. There are thousands of regional varieties and types available.

Butchery methods and laws

In the West, there are some minor differences in the butchering of meat from country to country, but in some other cultures there may be significant differences in the slaughter, aging and preparation of the carcass.

In Muslim countries, animals are ritually slaughtered in accordance with Islamic tradition, a method that involves cutting the throat of the animal and suspending it so that the blood drains out. The meat is known as halal meat,

Traditional dishes, such as hearty Roast Rib of Beef (above), are included in the recipe section along with contemporary ideas, such as Devilled Kidneys on Brioche Croûtes (right).

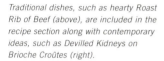

the word meaning "legal and allowed". This and other Islamic food customs have existed since the 7th century, taught by the prophet Muhammad, and strict Muslims will take care to buy meat only from halal butchers.

In Judaism, too, there are numerous food laws. Only animals that chew the cud and have cloven hooves can be eaten. All others, including pigs and horses, are considered unclean and are forbidden. All meat must be koshered before it is eaten, which means that it

must be slaughtered by cutting the animal's throat to let the blood drain. Meat and dairy products may not be eaten at the same meal, and in most countries only meat from the forequarter of the animal can be eaten.

New cuts of meat

The way that a butcher prepares a carcass to produce cuts of meat varies not only from country to country, but also sometimes from region to region,

and identical cuts often have a variety of different regional names. As a rule of thumb, the best joints come from the hindquarter and loin of an animal; in other words, those parts that have the least exercise. However, it is worth remembering that the tougher cuts are not only cheaper to buy, but they are also often extremely flavourful.

Using this book

The first part of this book gives a detailed guide to all the different types of meat, with useful information on equipment, buying and storing, as well as instructions on preparation and cooking methods.

The recipe section includes classic dishes from around the world as well as a range of modern recipes. You will find something here for every type of meal, whether it's a recipe for a romantic supper for two, something quick and easy to cook for family and friends, or an all-time classic, such as an impressive roast for a special occasion.

Left: Herb-crusted Rack of Lamb with Puy Lentils is just one example of how meat can fuse so well with exotic ingredients.

EQUIPMENT

Personal experience is the ideal guide to buying equipment. The novice cook or first-time kitchen owner is best advised to begin with a few basic items for preparing, cooking and serving, and then buy more equipment as required. Sophisticated appliances should be planned purchases. The important rule to remember is that the finest equipment is not a cure for bad basic cooking, but using the right tool often makes the job easier and quicker.

Usefulness

If the decision to buy is a difficult one, make a list of all tasks the equipment eases, then tick off tasks you already carry out by hand or with inferior tools. Next, tick off the things you want to do, but cannot because you do not have the right equipment.

Working space

With so many affordable large items of kitchenware readily available, it would be easy to fill the entire kitchen work surface, leaving barely enough space for a chopping board. Measure the equipment, then think about the space available and whether it is something that has to be left out permanently to be useful. Look at the availability of electric sockets. Check fittings, such

as clamps or wall-mounting brackets – for example, is the surface suitable for a mincer (grinder) to be clamped on it or is there space for a wall-mounted tool?

Storage

Cupboards (cabinets), drawers, shelves, hanging racks, tool trolleys or tool boxes are all useful. All options have good and bad points. Covered or closed storage (drawers or cupboards) are cleaner than open shelves or hanging racks, particularly in a small kitchen or near a hob (stovetop) where steam and odd splashes can be a problem.

Above: A steel for sharpening (top) is essential, along with a range of good-quality knives.

Below: Measuring cups and spoons

Over-filled drawers are not only very irritating, but they are also damaging to equipment and dangerous when sharp or pointed items, such as knives and skewers, are kept in them.

Equipment used often should be easily accessible – a hanging rack near the hob can be practical for small tools, such as large spoons and ladles, graters and strainers, that are used and washed regularly. Large, awkward or heavy items should be easy to lift and move, if necessary. Bad stacking causes damage, chipped edges and scratched surfaces. A handy tool box can be a great way of storing rarely used items, such as sausage-filling nozzles, mincer, pie funnel or individual pie tins (pans).

PREPARATION EQUIPMENT

Kitchen scales

There is a wide choice, from spring scales that are not particularly accurate to balance scales with weights (these can be precise) or digital scales, which vary in quality, but can be excellent, particularly for small amounts.

Measuring cups

American measuring cups are also available in other countries. They come in sizes from ¼ cup = 50ml/2fl oz to 1 cup = 250ml/8fl oz.

Measuring spoons

A set on a loop will not be lost as easily as separate spoons. These are essential for accurate measuring as they are calibrated in sizes from 1.5ml/¼tsp to 15ml/1 tbsp.

Knives

Select knives that are comfortable to hold and well balanced. Blades of high-grade stainless steel, fully forged with the tang running through the handle are strong and durable. It is better to have one good knife than 12 poor implements. Pay a premium price for a blade that will sharpen well. **A cook's knife** (sometimes called a chopping knife) with a blade about 20cm/8in long and **a paring knife**, with a 10cm/4in blade, are good basic choices. With these you will be able to carry out most techniques.

Knife sharpening and storing

A sharpener is essential for keeping knives sharp and useful; sharpen them regularly to keep the blade fine and smooth. Steel is the usual choice and better than many of the inexpensive sharpening devices. Electric knife sharpeners are available.

A stone is inexpensive and excellent for keeping knives sharp – available from hardware stores or Chinese supermarkets, look for a stone with a fine and coarse side. Start by sharpening on the coarse side, then grease the fine side with a little cooking oil to finish sharpening the blade.

Always wash and dry knives thoroughly after sharpening and before use. A knife block is useful for storing knives safely, it also helps to prevent damage caused when knives are jumbled together in a drawer.

A boning knife has a narrow, flexible blade, which bends easily for cutting around curved bones.
A carving knife with a 20–25cm/8–10in blade is useful for carving joints, and **a ham knife** with a 25cm/10in ridged blade is useful for carving thicker slices of meats, such as ham and pork.

Above: Plastic chopping boards

Meat cleaver

This heavy, wide-bladed knife is used for chopping meat bones and preparing Asian ingredients by authentic methods. It is also useful for finely chopping meat.

Above: Meat hammer and mallet

Scissors

Poultry scissors or shears are useful for cutting through bone, not just for poultry but also large pieces of meat. General kitchen scissors are useful for a multitude of tasks, such as snipping the rim of fat on bacon or a steak, or cutting bacon into fine strips.

Skewers

Metal skewers are useful for cooking meat kebabs. Skewers can also be used for piercing meat to check on cooking progress. Small skewers are useful when trussing smaller joints of meat. Wooden or bamboo skewers are used for some kebabs.

Meat hammer or mallet

Usually wooden, sometimes with metal ends, this is used to tenderize meat or to thin slices or steaks. Choose one with one flat side for beating and one dimpled side for tenderizing meat. A steak mallet is smaller than a meat hammer. It is made from metal and used to tenderize steak.

Chopping board

Wooden chopping boards are the traditional type. Sturdy plastic composite boards are more hygienic as they are not absorbent; however, they still need thorough scrubbing as the surface becomes scored with use. Sturdy plastic composite boards can be put in the dishwasher.

Above: General kitchen scissors, poultry shears and wooden and metal skewers

Above: Household string, clear film, foil and plastic bags

Mortar and pestle

This is used for crushing spices and grinding flavouring ingredients.

String

Buy fine string for cooking, to truss birds and tie joints of meat. Cook's shops sell high-quality, smooth string that does not leave tiny threads on the meat, but good string is available from stationers. Avoid "fluffy" string or coarse twine. Store the string in a plastic bag with cooking equipment to keep it clean and avoid handling it with dirty hands from gardening or similar messy tasks.

Kitchen foil

This is useful for covering meat to keep it moist and also to prevent it from becoming too brown during cooking.

Clear film

Also known as plastic wrap, this is useful for covering foods.

Plastic bags

Available in a variety of sizes, these are useful for storing raw and cooked meat and meat dishes in the freezer.

Plastic boxes with lids

These are invaluable for storing cooked dishes and individual portions of raw meat in the refrigerator or freezer.

Salt and pepper mills

For freshly ground black pepper and sea salt. Look for a pepper mill with a metal grinding mechanism (rather than plastic, which does not wear well). A pepper mill is also useful for favourite spices that are good coarsely ground, such as coriander.

Food processor

For chopping, grating, blending, slicing, beating, mincing (grinding) and many more culinary tasks. Select a processor with a bowl to suit your requirements, big enough to prepare the quantities in which you normally cook

Left: Mortar and pestle

and not too big to be of use for everyday amounts. Try to buy a food processor that will sit on your kitchen work surface, rather than one that has to be taken out of storage every time it is needed. Some large food processors have smaller bowls that fit inside the main container when processing small amounts. Look for an appliance that has a powerful motor, particularly useful when planning to mince (grind) or chop meat on a regular basis.

Mincer

Several types are available, from the traditional hand-cranked metal mincer, which clamps on to a work surface, to an electric model. All come with blades of various sizes, so that meat can be passed through a coarse blade first, then through a finer blade if required.

Above: Food processor

Right: Mincer

Left: This funnel is a simple sausage maker.

COOKING EQUIPMENT

Balloon whisk

Useful for whisking gravies and sauces, smoothing out lumps and bringing a gloss to the liquid.

Above: Balloon whisk

Timer

This is useful for accurately timing cooking.

Oven gloves

Buy heavy cotton mittens or the longer gauntlet type of glove. Use to protect your hands when handling hot dishes, tins and pans.

Metal tongs

Useful for lifting and turning small cuts of meat when cooking. The tongs shown above have a useful spring action.

Basting spoon

A large metal spoon for basting roasts and baked dishes during cooking.

Balloon baster

A huge plastic or metal dropper, with a heatproof balloon end for expelling air and squeezing in cooking

Above: Metal tongs

juices, which can be squirted over the top of the meat to baste. A balloon baster is also useful for transferring the excess fat from a roasting pan to a dish, for example, as when roasting fatty joints of meat.

Skimmer

A round, perforated, metal skimmer is ideal for skimming scum from stock.

Metal spatula or fish slice

These can be bought in various sizes and are useful for turning large pieces of meat during cooking.

Draining spoon

Perforated or with slots, this large, metal spoon is mainly used for removing meat from a pan or frying pan when browned, leaving the fat behind for cooking the next batch.

Sausage maker

There are several types. The cheapest are made of plastic and consist of a small funnel for passing the sausage meat (bulk sausage) into a tube for casing and a plunger to push it through. The more expensive machines are electric, but they work on the same principle. You can also make sausages using a piping (pastry) bag.

Meat hook

This is an item that is traditionally used for aging game but is also good for hanging meat.

Larding needle

A large, long needle with a ridged gripper at one end, used for threading strips of fat through lean joints of meat to ensure that the meat remains moist during cooking.

Trussing needle

This metal needle with a large eye is used for threading fine string through meat to keep it in shape during cooking.

Left, from top: Meat hooks, larding needle and trussing needle

Below: Basting spoon and metal spatula

Below: Skimmer

Above: A clockwork timer is inexpensive, yet extremely useful.

Left: Frying pans come in a range of sizes.

Griddle

These cast-iron cooking pans may be flat or ridged and are used for cooking on the hob (stovetop). Griddling, especially on a ridged pan, provides a healthy and attractive alternative to frying. The ridges keep the meat above fat that drips off, and they sear attractive marks on the surface of the meat as it cooks.

Left: Flat and ridged griddles

Pans

Three sizes of pan are useful, typically 16cm/6¼in, 19.5cm/7½in and 23cm/9in. Look for heavy, durable pans that distribute heat quickly and efficiently. The best are heavy stainless steel, with a core of copper and silver alloy in the base. Look for strong handles that do not conduct heat well and reinforced rims designed to pour cleanly. Look for a long guarantee from a reputable manufacturer and remember that high-quality, expensive pans will give a lifetime's service.

Non-stick coatings do not last so long as stainless steel. All-metal pans, which can be used in the oven as well as on the hob, are useful if you have a large oven. Buy the wrong pans and you will curse them every day, so it is worth taking plenty of time over the choice. Ask friends who share your cooking habits, read consumer reports and try out one pan before investing in the set.

Below: Pans

Above: Preserving pan

Frying pan

A good-quality, heavy frying pan with a non-stick coating is vital. Use for sealing joints and cooking small cuts.

Preserving pan

A traditional large and deep preserving pan can be useful for boiling ham.

Left: Stockpot

Roasting racks

Good roasting pans come with a rack, which sits inside the pan Place in the pan to allow heat to circulate around a joint evenly and fat to run off. Useful when cooking fatty meat.

Below: Roasting rack and pan

Casserole

An ovenproof cooking dish with a lid. Flameproof casseroles can be used on the hob, for browning ingredients, as well as braising in the oven.

Stockpot

A large, deep pan for making stock and cooking large cuts of meat. Heavy-duty stainless steel will last a lifetime. Look for a pan with small metal handles on both sides, then it will double as a huge ovenproof casserole.

Grill pan

A good-quality grill (broiler) pan will not buckle under fierce heat.

Roasting pans

Choose two heavy, deep pans to cook birds or joints of different sizes. They should be tough enough to withstand high heat and stovetop cooking as well as long, slow cooking without buckling and they should not rust. High-quality, heavy stainless steel or enamel tins are a good choice. Handles are a bonus and make lifting heavy roasts much easier. Covered roasting pans, with dimpled lids to encourage steam to condense and drip back into the pan avoid having to use expensive foil.

Roasting trays

The best roasting trays are made from heavy-duty aluminium. Again, select trays of different sizes to be able to best deal with different tasks.

Right: Oven and meat thermometers

Roasting bags

These are clear, ovenproof bags in which to roast meat. They are good for cooking small, rolled joints of meat. They not only keep in moisture, but also baste the food as it cooks. In addition, roasting bags help to keep the oven clean by preventing the hot juices splashing and spitting.

Meat thermometer

This is very useful for checking the cooking progress when roasting a joint of meat. Follow the manufacturer's instructions for use. Some types of thermometer are inserted into the raw joint, then placed in the oven with it. Others are inserted at the end of cooking, once the meat is removed from the oven. The point of the thermometer should be inserted into the middle of the thickest part of the joint.

Oven thermometer

Temperature gauges on ovens can be inaccurate. So it is a good idea to invest in a small, neat thermometer that will hang on the oven shelf and give an accurate reading.

SERVING EQUIPMENT

Ladles

Useful for serving sauces and gravies, as well as moist casseroles and stews.

Spiked meat platter

Metal platter, with short spikes in the middle to hold a joint in place while carving and (usually) a sunken rim into which fat or juices run and collect.

Carving fork

A sturdy, long-handled fork that is useful for holding joints of meat in place while carving joints.

Gravy skimming jug

This special jug (pitcher) has a double spout, so fat juices that form on the surface can be poured off before the gravy is poured out. This type of jug is also useful for skimming stock.

Sauceboat

Designed for serving gravies and sauces at the table. Make sure that it has a saucer to catch drips.

Above: Ladle

BUYING, PREPARING AND COOKING MEAT

This chapter includes essential information on meat from domesticated animals: beef and veal

from cows; lamb from sheep; and pork, bacon, gammon and ham from pigs. Sausages — both

fresh and cured — and cured meats are included, as is offal (innards).

Each section covers basic cuts and types, with information on nutrition, buying and storing.

Step-by-step techniques give detailed instructions for preparation techniques, as well as

information on every type of cooking method, from frying to roasting and stir-frying.

BEEF AND VEAL

Among the most varied of meats, beef provides a full-flavoured ingredient for stewing, succulent joints for roasting and tender steaks for grilling (broiling). In humble broths and peasant-style stews or extravagant dishes fit for banquets, the carcass includes cuts for all types of cooking, making it as good a choice for economical everyday meals as for dinner-party dishes.

Beef is eaten all over the world. From the British Sunday roast or the classic American burger to Russian Stroganoff, every country has its special dishes. Even though food and cooking are now multi-cultural, many traditional dishes have endured to become international favourites. Beef Wellington, succulent fillet (tenderloin) dressed with pâté and encased in puff pastry, also known as *boeuf en croûte*, stands out as one of the great dishes. Similarly, while the fashion for serving simple stews may fluctuate, some casseroles will always have a place on good menus. *Boeuf Bourguignonne*, made with little onions and mushrooms in red wine, or *osso bucco*, the Italian casserole of veal on the bone, are two good examples.

The same is true of Indian and South-east Asian cooking. Many curries, stir-fries, salads or pots of noodles based on beef feature not only in their home countries, but also in high-class dining rooms worldwide.

There are exceptions, and beef is not acceptable among all meat-eating cultures. For example, the cow is

regarded as a sacred animal by Hindus. It is appreciated for its milk and as a working animal, but not killed for its meat. In many African communities, cattle are prized possessions, given as a dowry with marrying daughters and accumulated rather than being reared for their meat.

Cattle have long been regarded as a source of milk or even for their blood, taken from the veins of the live animals and drunk as a source of nourishment, particularly by nomadic communities. Having a suitable temperament for herding and existing primarily on a diet of grass, these strong, useful animals were first domesticated in ancient Macedonia. They were inexpensive to buy and easy to keep, they provided milk and, ultimately, meat that was very good to eat.

Above: Some breeds, like these Highland cattle, are reared in only a few countries.

The beef we know today is far removed from the tough, stringy product from the carcass of an aged, working animal. Specific breeds have been developed over generations in different countries for the quantity and quality of meat they yield. For example, Aberdeen Angus and Hereford are well-known British breeds, and Charolais and Limousin are traditional French breeds. Although young dairy cows are used for meat, male cattle are the primary source, often castrated and always slaughtered young to yield a tender product. Breeding, rearing methods and environment, and ultimately the process of slaughtering and immediate management of the carcass all influence the quality of the meat.

Veal is not so universally popular as beef. In some countries it was at one time regarded as bland by comparison by some, then avoided because of general disapproval of rearing methods. In spite of a change of attitude and broader acceptance of veal, it is still not so popular as other meats. More humane rearing methods adopted in recent years are influencing choice, and veal is now available in supermarkets as well as from some butchers.

Left: New breeding methods for calves have made veal more acceptable, but it is still not so popular as other meats.

Nutrition

Not only does beef bring flavour to a meal, but it also makes a valuable contribution in terms of food value. Eaten in moderation, meat plays an excellent role in a healthy, well-balanced diet. Modern breeding has reduced the fat content of beef and meat is now sold trimmed of excess fat. It is worth remembering that the body needs some fat, so the aim should be to balance it with plenty of starchy foods, fresh fruit and vegetables.

Beef and veal are sources of high-quality protein. They provide all the essential amino acids required for growth as well as for maintaining the body. Beef is an excellent source of iron in a form that is easily absorbed by the body. It also provides zinc and other minerals and is an important source of many of the B vitamins.

Buying

Beef that is properly hung, for weeks rather than days, allowing time for the muscle to mature and the fat to develop, has a full flavour and becomes succulent and tender when cooked. Well-matured meat is a deep, rich, burgundy brown in colour, not bright red, and the fat is creamy rather than white. The best roasting joints are those from cuts with an even marbling of fat, which provides flavour and keeps the meat moist and juicy.

Look for meat that has been well butchered. The signs are cleanly cut meat, which is neat and evenly trimmed, with meat that follows the line of the muscle and bone. Bones should be smooth, without any sign of splinters. Smaller cuts, such as steaks, should be of uniform thickness so that they cook evenly in a similar length of time.

Right: Large roasting joints like this forerib of beef will keep in the refrigerator for up to five days before cooking.

Veal can be judged by its colour: the whiter the meat, the greater the proportion of milk in the diet of the calf. Pale meat is tender, with a delicate flavour. Older veal is pink or rosy pink, rather than white, and it often has a layer of creamy-white fat. If it is brown, veal is either very old or very stale. Veal has little fat, and joints are often larded before roasting to keep them moist.

Storing

Beef and veal should be kept on a low shelf in the refrigerator, below and away from cooked foods and ingredients that are to be eaten raw.

As a general rule, when buying pre-packed meat, always check and observe the use-by date on the packet. Pre-packed meat, which is securely sealed, should be stored in its packaging. If the packaging is damaged and there is any danger of meat juices escaping, or if the meat is bought loose and wrapped in a bag, transfer it to a covered dish in the refrigerator.

Above: Loose minced beef is best cooked on the day it is bought.

The dish must be large enough to contain any juices, and the lid should cover it completely.

As a guide to meat that is not pre-packed, minced (ground) meat and small cuts of veal are best eaten on the day you buy them, but joints, chops and steaks will keep for up to three days and larger joints for up to five days.

Beef and veal freeze well, particularly smaller pieces. Store tightly wrapped, individual portions of veal for up to six months and beef for up to one year. Thoroughly thaw the meat before cooking. Put the meat in a large dish to catch drips and thaw slowly in the refrigerator overnight. Never re-freeze raw meat that has once been thawed.

Beef and BSE

Bovine spongiform encephalopathy, a disease found in cattle in the 1980s, is thought to be the result of feed manufactured from sheep and cattle carcasses. The growth in the number of cattle with the disease resulted in a review of cattle rearing, slaughtering and butchering, and the use of cattle food generated from animal carcasses has now been banned. Some types of offal and beef on the bone were withdrawn from sale in some countries, but it is likely that these bans will be lifted.

*Right:
Sirloin can
be roasted or
cut into steaks for
frying or grilling.*

Butchering techniques differ according to country and regional traditions. Many larger supermarkets or good butchers offer a wide selection of international cuts. Cuts from the top of the animal, along the middle of the back, are tender because they are from muscles, that perform comparatively light work. These include the most expensive cuts, which can be cooked by grilling (broiling) and frying as well as by roasting. Cuts from the neck, shoulders and lower legs, the parts of the animal that work hardest, are tougher, coarse in texture and less expensive than the prime cuts. For tender results, they require longer cooking by moist, gentle methods. However, when well cooked, these cuts have an excellent flavour. The following is a guide to the basic beef cuts.

THE BASIC CUTS OF BEEF

There is a wide choice of beef, the result not only of basic butchering techniques, but also of advanced preparation. As well as traditional small cuts and large joints, boned, sliced, diced and trimmed meat is available.

Check the labels on packed meats, as they include a guide to cooking or the method for which the meat is best suited. The butcher or person weighing meat at the loose meat counter in the supermarket will be trained to provide information on the joints or particular prepared meats on offer. It is worth asking their advice, especially as they will be aware of particularly good buys.

Sirloin

Also known as best end loin, the sirloin can also be cut into steaks: entrecôte (sirloin), porterhouse and T-bone. This is a lean, tender cut from the back of the animal for roasting in joints or grilling and frying as steaks.

Entrecôte steak

A steak cut from the sirloin.

*Above: Entrecôte
steaks are cut from the
sirloin.*

*Below: Chateaubriand is a
cut from the centre of
the fillet.*

*Left: New
York steak*

Porterhouse steak

Traditionally a large steak cut from the sirloin, but sometimes used for steaks cut from the rib of beef.

Forerib

A high-quality cut available on the bone or boned and rolled for roasting as a joint or cut into thick slices for grilling or frying.

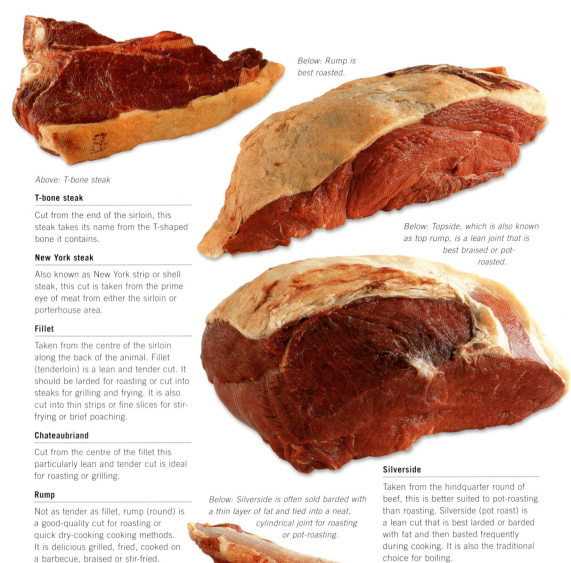

Below: Rump is best roasted.

Above: T-bone steak

T-bone steak

Cut from the end of the sirloin, this steak takes its name from the T-shaped bone it contains.

New York steak

Also known as New York strip or shell steak, this cut is taken from the prime eye of meat from either the sirloin or porterhouse area.

Fillet

Taken from the centre of the sirloin along the back of the animal. Fillet (tenderloin) is a lean and tender cut. It should be larded for roasting or cut into steaks for grilling and frying. It is also cut into thin strips or fine slices for stir-frying or brief poaching.

Chateaubriand

Cut from the centre of the fillet this particularly lean and tender cut is ideal for roasting or grilling.

Rump

Not as tender as fillet, rump (round) is a good-quality cut for roasting or quick dry-cooking cooking methods. It is delicious grilled, fried, cooked on a barbecue, braised or stir-fried.

Topside

Also known as top rump or pot roast in the US, this cut is taken from the round of beef. Available boned and rolled ready for roasting, it is also good braised. Topside is quite lean so it is best larded or barded with a little fat before cooking and basted frequently during cooking.

Below: Topside, which is also known as top rump, is a lean joint that is best braised or pot-roasted.

Below: Silverside is often sold barded with a thin layer of fat and tied into a neat, cylindrical joint for roasting or pot-roasting.

Silverside

Taken from the hindquarter round of beef, this is better suited to pot-roasting than roasting. Silverside (pot roast) is a lean cut that is best larded or barded with fat and then basted frequently during cooking. It is also the traditional choice for boiling.

Shin

This is a tough cut of beef that needs long, slow cooking, preferably stewing. Shin (shank) is a lean cut with a good flavour and is often sold boned and cut for stewing.

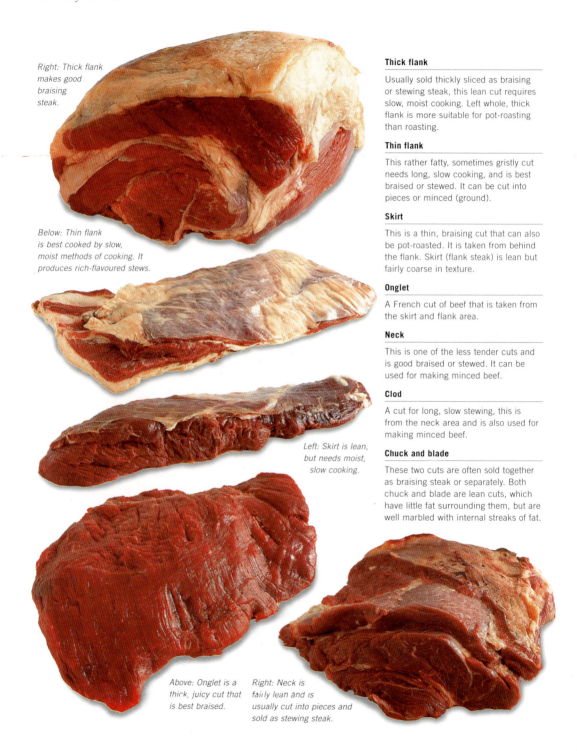

Right: Thick flank makes good braising steak.

Below: Thin flank is best cooked by slow, moist methods of cooking. It produces rich-flavoured stews.

Left: Skirt is lean, but needs moist, slow cooking.

Above: Onglet is a thick, juicy cut that is best braised.

Right: Neck is fairly lean and is usually cut into pieces and sold as stewing steak.

Thick flank

Usually sold thickly sliced as braising or stewing steak, this lean cut requires slow, moist cooking. Left whole, thick flank is more suitable for pot-roasting than roasting.

Thin flank

This rather fatty, sometimes gristly cut needs long, slow cooking, and is best braised or stewed. It can be cut into pieces or minced (ground).

Skirt

This is a thin, braising cut that can also be pot-roasted. It is taken from behind the flank. Skirt (flank steak) is lean but fairly coarse in texture.

Onglet

A French cut of beef that is taken from the skirt and flank area.

Neck

This is one of the less tender cuts and is good braised or stewed. It can be used for making minced beef.

Clod

A cut for long, slow stewing, this is from the neck area and is also used for making minced beef.

Chuck and blade

These two cuts are often sold together as braising steak or separately. Both chuck and blade are lean cuts, which have little fat surrounding them, but are well marbled with internal streaks of fat.

These cuts benefit from long, slow cooking to develop the flavour of the meat and give tender results.

Thick rib

Also known as top rib, this cut is taken from beneath the chuck and blade above the brisket. It is often boned and rolled, but it is best roasted with the bone in. It can also be cut into steaks and either pot-roasted or braised.

Thin rib

Also known as flat rib, this comes from behind the thick rib, below the forerib and above the brisket. It is a cut for pot-roasting or braising.

Brisket

Taken from the fore end of the animal, just below the shoulder. This is a fairly tough cut that has a comparatively high proportion of fat. It is a well-flavoured cut that tastes best when pot-roasted, braised or stewed, but may also be salted or spiced.

Leg

This tough cut comes from the back legs of the animal. It is usually sold cut into thick slices cut horizontally through the central bone and needs long, slow cooking, such as stewing or braising. When cooked, the meat is richly flavoured and gelatinous.

Minced beef

The paler the colour, the higher the fat content, so look for dark beef, which has a high proportion of lean meat. Use minced (ground) beef for meat sauces and burgers.

Above: Chuck steak is one of the best meats for stewing.

Above: Thick rib is sold with and without the bone.

Left: Thin rib is excellent pot-roasted.

Above: Blade is usually boned and cut into thick slices. It is well marbled with fat and, cooked slowly, produces rich-tasting stews.

Above: Brisket is often boned and rolled.

THE BASIC CUTS OF VEAL

There is an increasingly wide range of veal cuts available from butchers and larger supermarkets. There are large cuts suitable for roasting and braising and smaller cuts for the quicker cooking methods of frying, griddling and grilling (broiling). The following is a guide to the basic cuts of veal.

Above: Fillet is usually cut into escalopes.

Above: Breast has an excellent flavour.

Above: Veal chops, which resemble T-bone steaks, are from the loin and good for grilling or frying.

Right: This large, prime veal joint for roasting is a combination of loin and fillet and is available from good butchers.

Above: Leg, a large, lean cut that is often roasted.

Fillet

This is a lean, boneless cut taken from the hindquarters. Fillet (tenderloin) is usually sliced crossways into thin escalopes (scallops) and then sautéed, but it can also be roasted whole.

Breast

This cut can be roasted on the bone, or boned, stuffed, rolled and roasted, or cut up into riblets for grilling.

Chops

Taken from the loin, these are on the bone, and they are usually grilled (broiled), griddled or pan-fried.

Left: Knuckle is the bonier end of the hind leg and is often cut into thick slices and used to make the rich Italian stew, osso bucco.

Right: Shoulder of veal is often sold boned and rolled.

Knuckle

The end of the hind leg, this is very bony and used mainly for boiling or stewing, but can also be braised. It is usually sold cut crossways into thick slices.

Cutlets

Taken from the neck end of the loin, these are usually griddled, grilled (broiled) or pan-fried.

Shoulder

Also called the oyster, this can be boned, stuffed and rolled and makes an excellent, not-too-expensive joint for roasting. Shoulder can also be cut into chunks for stewing or as a pie filling.

Best end of neck

Known in the US as cross rib, this is usually sold on the bone for roasting and is juicy and tender. Ask the butcher to remove the chine bone so that it can be carved more easily.

Leg

A good-quality cut for roasting. This large, tender cut is often boned and stuffed.

Loin

Taken from the back of the animal and available either on the bone or boned and rolled. This lean, tender cut is ideal for roasting.

Right: Best end of neck is one of the tougher cuts of veal and so is better pot-roasted, braised or stewed.

Left: Cutlets are cut from the neck end of the loin and are good cooked quickly by grilling, griddling or frying.

Wines to serve with beef and veal

Beef is a big powerful red meat that will stand a big powerful red wine. The classic wines of Bordeaux – made mainly from Cabernet Sauvignon, Cabernet Franc and Merlot grapes – complement beef perfectly. Try a smooth St Emilion or Margaux with a roast or the heavier reds from the Médoc or Graves with a robust stew.

Full-bodied Italian red wines are also good with beef stews. Alternatively, try the smooth Merlots from Bulgaria and the Australian reds made from Cabernet Sauvignon, Shiraz, Grenache and Pinot Noir grapes. The complex Cabernet Sauvignons from the Napa Valley, Sonoma County and Santa Cruz go well with beef and veal. The soft, fruity reds made from Merlot and Cabernet Sauvignon in Washington State are a good choice for pan-fried veal.

South Africa's traditionally burly reds made from Pinotage, Pinot Noir, Merlot, Shiraz and Cabernet Sauvignon stand up well to beef.

The sophisticated Cabernet Sauvignons from Chile and the earthy reds – made from Malbec, Merlot and Cabernet Sauvignon – from Argentina are also worth trying with beef and veal.

PREPARING BEEF AND VEAL

Boning

Depending on the cut, beef and veal can be cooked on or off the bone. As with other types of meat, boneless joints are easier to carve and serve. They can also be stuffed or cut up, for example into cubes or dice. Butchers are always ready to bone meat given notice and they are best equipped for the task, with the right equipment and skills.

However, it is useful to know how to tackle the task. Whatever the cut, there are a few basic principles to follow: use a sharp knife, preferably one with a fine, flexible blade as it will follow the contours of the bones easily. Follow the shape of the bone, removing the maximum amount of meat and cutting around it, rather than slicing into it.

1 To bone a rib of beef, follow the rib bones, working down from the tops of the bones. Follow the curve of the bone with the knife, easing the meat away from the bone as it becomes free.

2 Carefully cut through the cartilage around the base, keeping the eye of the meat as whole and neat as possible. Then remove the bone. Finally, trim off any excess fat from the boned joint.

Barding and larding

These are methods of introducing fat to very lean joints, to keep them moist and succulent during the cooking process and also to add flavour.

Barding

This is simply wrapping fat around or over lean meat; thin slices of pork or beef fat can be used. This is often obvious on lean, rolled joints bought from the supermarket where the meat is wrapped in a separate coating of fat. Streaky (fatty) bacon can also be used for barding. The outer covering of fat bastes the meat, preventing it from drying out before it is cooked through.

Larding

This involves more preparation and is the technique of threading strips of pork fat through lean meat to keep it moist from the inside as the fat melts during roasting. The strips of fat, or lardons, can be rolled in herbs or spices before being threaded through the meat to add extra flavours to the meat.

A larding needle is used; with some less tender cuts or if the needle is blunt, it may be necessary to pierce holes through the meat with a skewer first before inserting the strips of fat.

A larding needle has a gripping device, instead of a hole, to hold the fat. For meats that will be cooked by slow, moist methods, insert the needle, following the grain of the meat. Attach a strip of fat to the needle, then push the needle through the meat. Lard the meat at regular intervals to keep it evenly moist during cooking. For meats that are to be roasted, thread the strips of fat into the outside of the meat in long stitches.

Tying a boneless joint

A boneless joint, such as sirloin or topside (pot roast), is best tied before roasting. This helps to keep it in shape and promotes even cooking. The joint may be stuffed first, if required – make sure that the cavity is large enough to contain the stuffing so that it is not squeezed out when the joint is tied. Fine string is used for tying – this is available from good cook's shops and larger supermarkets, or alternatively fine parcel string can be used. It is a good idea to use special cooking string and store it in a plastic bag or box so that it is kept clean.

1 Roll, fold or arrange the meat into a neat shape, then tie a piece of fine string lengthways around the joint. Pull the ends tightly (it needs to be fairly tight as the meat will shrink during cooking) and secure the string with a double knot.

2 Tie more string around the joint at regular intervals, about 2.5cm/1in apart, knotting and trimming the ends as you go. Try to ensure that you apply even pressure when tying each length of string to keep the meat in a neat, even shape and to avoid squeezing the meat more in some places than others.

Trimming and slicing fillet

Before cutting steaks, to create a neat eye of meat, remove the chain muscle running along the side.

1 When the small chain muscle has been removed, cut away the sinewy membrane that held it in place.

2 Cut the fillet (tenderloin) into 2cm/¾in thick slices. Cut slightly thicker slices at the narrower end and pound them with a meat mallet to flatten them to the same size as the wider slices.

Trimming steak

Although a little fat gives good flavour, a thick rim of fat does not cook well in the time it takes to grill (broil) steak.

1 Trim the outer layer of fat, leaving no more than 5mm/¼in next to the meat.

2 Use sharp, kitchen scissors to snip the fat around the steak at 2.5cm/1in intervals around the edge. This helps to prevent the steak curling up during frying or grilling (broiling).

Cutting meat for braising or stewing

Tougher cuts of meat, such as braising or stewing steak, cook evenly and more quickly if they are cut into thick slices or small even-size cubes for cooking.

1 Trim the meat, cutting off the excess fat and any gristle, membranes or sinew from the meat.

2 Cut the meat across the grain into 2.5cm/1in thick slices, using a large, sharp knife. Slices of braising steak can be either braised or casseroled. Braising or stewing steak can also be cut into cubes (see step 4).

3 To cut the meat into cubes, first cut the slices lengthways into thick strips.

4 Cut the strips of meat crossways into 2.5cm/1in cubes.

Tenderizing steak

Pounding meat breaks down its tissues and helps to give a tender result.

Place the steak on a chopping board and cover it with greaseproof (waxed) paper or lay the meat between two sheets of greaseproof paper. Pound evenly with a meat mallet.

COOK'S TIP

Pounding meat is especially important with thicker pieces of tender cuts. If you don't have a meat mallet, use the base of a heavy pan, or a wooden rolling pin. Ensure that you beat the meat evenly.

Mincing

When you mince (grind) meat at home, it means you can select the cut and trim off excess fat first. Stewing or braising cuts are ideal, especially for making long-cooked meat sauces, but rump (round) or fillet steak can be minced for making burgers and similar dishes. A food processor can be used: this gives finely ground meat, rather than the coarser texture. Trim the meat and cut it into small cubes, then process it in small batches for even results, pulsing the power on and off. Do not over-process.

To use a traditional mincer (grinder), trim the meat and cut it into pieces, then feed it into the top of the mincer, while turning the handle. Use a coarse blade for long-simmered sauces and a medium one for meat loaves or meatballs. For a finer texture, pass the meat through a coarse blade first, then pass it through a fine blade.

Alternatively, cubed steak can be chopped finely. This is particularly good for tender frying cuts. Use a pair of very sharp knives, one in each hand, and a rhythmic chopping action. Use the flat blades to bring in the meat from the sides so that it is all evenly chopped.

Steak tartare

This is a dish of uncooked, hand-minced steak, seasoned and flavoured to individual taste and served with a raw egg yolk. It is vital that both meat and egg are perfectly fresh and bought from reliable suppliers. The meat must be prepared at home to avoid any risk of cross-contamination.

1 Finely mince 450g/1lb fillet steak by chopping it with a pair of very sharp knives.

2 Stir in 1 finely chopped small onion, 30ml/2 tbsp chopped fresh parsley, salt and black pepper.

3 Arrange the steak in mounds on 4 chilled plates. Make a hollow in the middle of each. Place 1 egg yolk in each hollow and serve.

COOKING BEEF AND VEAL

Pan-frying

This is the traditional cooking method for steaks, such as sirloin and fillet, and is also good for veal chops. Use a heavy, non-stick pan. Cook in the minimum of fat, then add flavoured butter when serving, if you like. Butter burns easily, so heat the oil in the pan first and add the butter just before the meat, to avoid this.

1 Use kitchen paper to grease the frying pan with a little sunflower oil.

2 Heat the pan until it is very hot before adding a knob (pat) of butter.

3 The butter should melt immediately. Add the steak or chop and cook for the required time (see right).

4 Use a metal spatula to transfer the steak to a warm plate.

Cooking times for pan-fried beef
The cooking time depends on the cut and on how well done you like it.
For very rare fillet (tenderloin) steak, cut about 2.5cm/1in thick, allow 1 minute each side; for rump (round) allow 2 minutes each side.
For rare steak, allow 2 minutes each side for fillet; 3 minutes for rump.
For medium fillet steak, allow 2–3 minutes; allow 2–4 minutes for rump. **For well-done steak**, allow 3 minutes, then reduce the heat for 5–10 minutes.

Dry-frying beef

The method varies according to the meat. Lean beef, such as steak, is cooked in a very hot pan smeared with a little oil. High-fat meat is fried over a high heat so that the fat it contains melts and seeps out. The fat can then be discarded or used for cooking.

1 Preheat a frying pan or flameproof casserole. Add the meat and cook over a high heat; stir-fry minced (ground) beef; separate strips; or turn steaks.

Steak *au poivre*

This classic dish is made by coating fillet steak with crushed peppercorns, which flavour it, protect it as it is pan-fried and give a crunchy texture.

1 In a small mortar using a pestle, coarsely crush 30–45ml/2–3 tbsp black peppercorns.

2 Tip the crushed peppercorns on to a plate and press each piece of steak firmly into them to coat both sides evenly.

3 Grease a frying pan with a little oil, then heat until very hot. Add a knob of butter, followed by the steak as soon as the butter has melted. Cook until the steak is well browned and cooked (see cooking times for pan-frying, left).

Pan-frying veal

There are many tender cuts of veal suitable for pan-frying. Escalopes (scallops) from the fillet are the classic cut for this method.

1 Place the veal between two sheets of clear film (plastic wrap) or greaseproof (waxed) paper, or on a chopping board, and cover with clear film. Use the flat side of a meat mallet or a rolling pin firmly, but gently to beat the veal out thinly and evenly. Repeat with the remaining escalopes.

2 Use a heavy frying pan, preferably non-stick, and heat it until it is very hot. Smear with enough butter and oil to prevent the meat from sticking. Add the veal escalopes when the fat is sizzling and cook for 1–2 minutes.

3 Turn the escalopes over and cook for 1–2 minutes on the second side. Serve immediately, with the pan juices poured over, or make a simple sauce (see the Cook's Tip below).

COOK'S TIP
To make a simple sauce, remove the veal and keep warm. Add a splash of sherry, simmer to reduce by half, then add double (heavy) cream and season.

Stir-frying

This is a fast method of cooking tender meat. The meat should be cut into thin slices across the grain, and then the slices cut into fine, long strips. Use rump (round) or fillet (tenderloin) steak. Also look out for steak sold prepared especially for stir-frying.

1 Heat a wok or large, heavy frying pan to smoking point and then add a little oil.

2 Add the meat in batches and cook over a high heat, stirring constantly to cook the meat evenly.

3 Remove the first batch before adding more meat. If too much meat is added at once, the temperature drops, the strips of meat do not cook quickly and their juices seep out, then they braise in the juices.

Griddling

This is a fashionable, healthy method of cooking, suitable for steaks, such as rump, sirloin and fillet. A ridged, cast-iron pan allows the fat to drain away into the grooves while the meat cooks. The meat is seared with the pattern of the hot ridges. A non-stick griddle is useful for cooking with the minimum of extra fat.

1 Preheat the griddle until it is almost smoking. Brush the meat very lightly with a little vegetable or sunflower oil, which are very light and will not flavour the meat.

2 Lay the meat on the griddle and cook following times for grilling (broiling).

3 Metal tongs are useful for turning steaks halfway through cooking.

Grilling beef

This is a quick way of cooking lean meats, such as rump, sirloin or fillet steak because the fat drips away during the cooking process. Preheat the grill (broiler) for 5 minutes, until very hot. The fierce heat quickly cooks the surface of the meat to seal in the juices. If the grill is not hot enough, the meat cooks slowly, allowing the juices to seep out. Cooking the meat quickly keeps it moist and tender. The steaks should be cut to the same thickness to ensure even cooking.

1 Brush the steak with a little light vegetable oil or melted butter on both sides to keep it moist during cooking. Season the steak well with salt and freshly ground black pepper, then place the steaks on the grill rack.

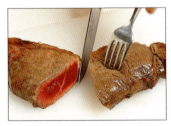

2 To cook the steak until very rare (*bleu*) using fillet steaks cut 2.5–3.5cm/ 1–1¼in thick, allow about 1 minute on each side; for rump steaks allow about 2 minutes on each side.

COOK'S TIP

Use a light oil, such as vegetable or sunflower oil, for brushing the steak. If you use a heavier oil, such as olive oil, it detracts from the flavour of the meat.

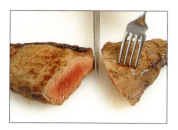

3 For rare steak *(saignant):* increase the time for fillet to 2 minutes each side; 3 minutes for rump.

4 For medium steak *(à point):* allow 2–3 minutes each side for fillet, 2–4 minutes for rump.

5 For well-done steak *(bien cuit):* allow 3 minutes on each side, then reduce the grill setting and allow a further 5–10 minutes, turning the steak once or twice, until the meat is firm and brown.

Right: Flavoured butters are excellent for serving with steak – the pats of butter melt on the hot steak to form a simple, yet delicious sauce.

Barbecuing

The barbecue should be lit about 30 minutes before cooking. The coals are ready when they are grey and ashen on the surface – this is when they are hot, but not flaming. They will cook the meat quickly and evenly. The rack must not be too near the coals. If the coals are too hot or the rack too near them, the meat will burn on the outside before it is cooked to taste in the middle. Brush the barbecue rack lightly with a little sunflower oil before laying the food on it.

Marinating is a good way of bringing flavour to meat before grilling, griddling, pan-frying or cooking on a barbecue, and it helps to keep very dry cuts moist during cooking. Lengthy marinating also helps to tenderize the meat. Kebabs can be marinated once threaded on skewers, to save time when ready to cook, or the cubes of meat can be marinated separately for an hour or two before threading.

The marinade can be used to baste the kebabs or meat before and during cooking. Regular basting promotes even cooking and prevents the meat or other ingredients from drying out.

Flavoured butters

One of the simplest ways of dressing grilled, griddled, pan-fried or barbecued steak is by adding a pat of flavoured butter. Beat one of the flavouring ingredients below into 225g/8oz softened, unsalted (sweet) butter. Chill until fairly firm, then roll into a cylinder in greaseproof (waxed) paper and wrap in clear film (plastic wrap). The flavoured butter can be stored in the refrigerator for up to 2 days. Slice the butter and place on the hot steak before serving.

Garlic butter Add 2 plump finely chopped garlic cloves.
Parsley butter Add 30ml/2 tbsp chopped fresh parsley.
Mixed herb butter Add 30ml/2 tbsp chopped fresh herbs.
Lemon butter Add 30ml/2 tbsp lemon juice and the grated rind of 1 lemon. Lemon juice and rind also go well with garlic or fresh parsley or a mixture of both.
Chilli butter Add ½ –1 fresh red seeded and chopped chilli.
Shallot butter Sauté 1 chopped shallot in butter, add 15ml/1 tbsp red wine and cook for 5 minutes. Cool, then beat into the butter.

Stewing, braising and casseroling

These are long, slow and moist methods of cooking either in the oven or on the hob (stovetop). The meat is simmered at a low temperature in liquid – wine, water, beer or stock. This is ideal for tough, inexpensive cuts, such as shin (shank), leg, brisket, thin flank, or chuck and blade. Stewing steak needs longer cooking than braising steak.

1 Trim off any excess fat and cut the meat into 2.5cm/1in cubes.

2 Toss the meat in seasoned flour, shaking off any excess. This coating browns to give the casserole a good flavour and thickens the cooking liquid.

3 Heat 30ml/2 tbsp sunflower oil in a flameproof casserole. Add the meat in batches and cook over a high heat.

4 When the meat is well browned on all sides, use a slotted spoon to remove it before adding the next batch to the casserole. If necessary, heat a little extra sunflower oil in the casserole before adding more meat.

5 Add sliced or chopped onions and other vegetables to the remaining fat and juices in the casserole and cook, stirring occasionally, for 5 minutes.

6 Return the meat to the casserole, add herbs, then pour in the cooking liquid. Stir to loosen all the cooking residue from the base of the pan and heat until simmering. Simmer gently on the hob or cook in the oven until tender. The casserole may be covered for the entire length of the cooking or uncovered towards the end to allow excess liquid to evaporate.

Pot-roasting

This long, slow method of cooking is ideal for slightly tough joints, such as brisket, thick flank and topside (pot roast). The meat is cooked in a covered pot on a bed of vegetables with a small quantity of liquid, which creates a moist environment. This produces very succulent results.

1 Heat a little sunflower oil in a large, flameproof casserole until very hot. Add the meat and cook over a high heat, turning frequently, until browned on all sides. Remove the meat from the pan.

2 Stir in onions, leeks and root vegetables, then cook, stirring, for a few minutes. Replace the meat on top of the vegetables and pour in a little liquid, such as stock, wine or beer. Cover and cook gently on the hob or in the oven until the meat is tender.

COOK'S TIP

One of the easiest ways of coating cubes of meat evenly in seasoned flour is to put the seasoned flour in a large plastic bag. Add a couple of cubes of meat at a time and shake gently until the meat is evenly coated in flour. Remove the coated cubes of meat and transfer to a plate before adding the next batch.

Roasting beef

Large joints give best results, allowing time for the outside of the meat to brown and the fat to melt and become crisp before the centre of the joint is overcooked. Forerib (either on or off the bone) or sirloin are good cuts for roasting. Fillet (tenderloin) can be roasted, but it is very lean and should be larded, then basted during cooking.

Roasting times for beef
Weigh the joint and calculate the cooking time as follows:
On the bone
For rare beef: 20 minutes per 450g/1lb at 180°C/350°F/Gas 4, plus 20 minutes.
For a medium result: 25 minutes per 450g/1lb, plus 25 minutes.
For well-done beef: 30 minutes per 450g/1lb, plus 30 minutes.
Off the bone
For rare beef: 15 minutes per 450g/1lb at 180°C/350°F/Gas 4, plus 15 minutes.
For a medium result: 20 minutes per 450g/1lb, plus 20 minutes.
For well-done beef: 25 minutes per 450g/1lb, plus 25 minutes.

Roasting times for veal
Allow 25 minutes per 450g/1lb at 180°C/350°F/Gas 4, plus an extra 25 minutes, for veal on or off the bone.

Roasting techniques

There are two methods: either place the cold joint in the oven or sear it first. When cooking a very large joint, it is easier to place it in a roasting pan, fat-side up, and roast for the calculated time. The comparatively long cooking allows plenty of time for the fat to melt and brown. Alternatively, with a medium-size joint, browning the fat first on the hob (stovetop) gives a better result, as the cooking time is not long enough to cook the fat thoroughly. This method helps to prevent uneven shrinkage, which can make a joint irregular in shape.

1 Preheat the oven to 180°C/350°F/Gas 4. Heat a little oil in a frying pan and sear the joint of beef on all sides, particularly the fat. Season well and place on a rack in a roasting pan, fat-side up, then transfer to the oven.

2 Roast the meat for the calculated time. A meat thermometer is useful for checking progress and to determine when the joint is cooked. Heat the spike of the thermometer in very hot water, then insert it into the thickest part of the joint to check the temperature: 60°C/140°F indicates that the meat is rare, 70°C/158°F is a medium result and 75°C/167°F is well done.

3 Cover with foil; leave for 10 minutes before carving. This allows the temperature to even out and the fibres to relax, making the meat easier to carve.

Carving a rolled joint

When the cooked joint has been allowed to stand and relax for 10 minutes, remove the string before carving.

Use a carving fork to hold the joint firmly in position, then cut the meat into slices using a gentle sawing action. When carving this type of joint, the meat can be cut into even, thin slices.

Carving rib of beef

1 Allow the cooked joint to stand for 10 minutes to relax, then place it on a board or spiked meat platter and hold it firmly in place with a carving fork. Cut down between the meat and the ribs to remove the meat from the bones.

2 Set the bones aside. Turn the joint on its side and carve even slices across the grain of the meat.

LAMB

This rich meat is savoured as succulent roasts, delicious on chargrilled kebabs and inimitable in full-flavoured stews or casseroles. Matched by robust herbs or aromatic spices and served with piquant or zesty accompaniments, lamb features in all cuisines. From Morocco there are spicy tagines of lamb cooked with fruit and served with couscous; throughout the Middle East lamb is cooked with rice or other grains and fruit to make intense pilaffs; Indian cooks prepare koftas with minced (ground) lamb or saffron-soaked roasts and cream-enriched kormas from tender cuts. Potato-topped pies, dainty cutlets or noisettes are typical Western favourites.

These and other lamb dishes span all cultures and occasions. The meat from sheep has always been a democratic food, found on the plates of the poor and rich alike. In countries where many peasant populations rely on vegetables, grains and pulses for their meagre diet, lamb is often the sacrificial animal, offered by the rich on festive occasions and shared with the less wealthy.

Historically, sheep were mainly reared for their products – milk and wool. Sheep were central to the whole way of life of many early communities, and they were considered so vital for wool production in Elizabethan England that there was a ban on killing them. In Asia, however, where sheep were first domesticated, the meat was also eaten.

Above: The meat of sheep from New Zealand is internationally renowned.

Left: Different countries have their own particular breeds. These dark-coated sheep are from the Scottish Hebrides.

Modern breeds and types

Farming and modern rearing have introduced breeds that are well removed from the scrawny animals that would have provided modest amounts of tough, strong-flavoured meat centuries ago. Tastes have changed comparatively recently and the mutton that was a choice meat in Victorian times is too strong for contemporary palates.

Countries have their particular breeds, for example fat-tailed sheep are reared in the Middle East for their long tails (usually docked from other breeds and in other countries). Wales is famous for flavoursome lamb and the South Downs in England is an area of excellent grazing and produces high-quality meat. The salt marshes of Brittany in northern France are home to *pré-salé* lamb, which has a distinct and tasty flavour. New Zealand and Australia are internationally known as excellent sources of lamb, with New Zealand exporting high-quality meat.

Young lambs, killed before they are weaned, yield delicate, pale meat known as sucking lamb or *agneau de lait* in France, where two categories are produced depending on maturity. Milk-fed lamb is also appreciated in Italy. Meat from grazing animals is more common, usually from four months old and up to one year. Mutton comes from older sheep, over a year and onwards. Just as sucking lamb is not widely eaten, old-fashioned mutton is not readily available or popular, but it can be purchased from specialist butchers. Before refrigeration and modern storage methods, lamb and mutton were salted in the same way as pork. Now a gourmet "find", salted lamb or mutton ham is available from specialist suppliers. Smoked lamb is not widely available, but it is prepared when good lamb is available and small specialist smokers have space available for its preparation.

Flavour enhancers

Just as Yorkshire pudding and similar starchy puddings were served to satisfy hunger and make a little beef go a long way, so thousands of years ago, bitter herbs were first added to lamb in the hope that this would make it less palatable, such that a little would be eaten in modest amounts. However, the sharp flavours were found to enhance and complement the lamb. Over the years, mint or other herbs combined with vinegar, were sweetened with sugar to become an appropriate condiment.

Sweet, sour and sharp flavours are long established seasonings for rich or fatty meats. While mint sauce is a classic accompaniment for Western-style roast lamb, tangy, natural (plain) yogurt is popular for marinating the meat of older animals before cooking it with spices, Indian style, or combining it with herbs for Mediterranean dishes. Marinating in yogurt, vinegar, lemon juice or tamarind juice also helps to tenderize sturdy mutton before cooking.

Nutrition

Although lamb is traditionally a fatty meat, particularly from some of the mountain breeds, notably Welsh lamb, the fat content depends on the breed

Below: Lamb noisettes and cutlets are examples of good lamb, with their fine-grained pink meat and creamy-white, firm fat.

and the rearing methods. The meat available now is no longer so fatty as it was in the past, and sheep farmers are rearing leaner animals that still have excellent flavour.

Along with other meats, lamb is primarily a high-quality protein food. It is an excellent source of iron in a form that is readily absorbed by the body and it is also a good source of zinc. Meat, including lamb, also provides an important source of the B vitamins and minerals, including copper, manganese and selenium.

For a healthy balance, serve modest portions of meat for everyday meals, adding plenty of starchy foods, such as potatoes, bread, rice and pasta, and lots of vegetables and fruit. Lamb is splendid in casseroles with vegetables and pulses, such as pumpkin, green beans, haricot (navy) beans and potatoes. Flageolet beans (small cannellini) are delicious with roast or grilled (broiled) lamb.

Above: Joints of lamb will keep in the refrigerator for up to five days.

Buying

Meat from milk-fed baby lamb is very pale and looks rather like veal; meat from sheep less than one year old has slightly darker pink flesh; meat from sheep more than one year old is known as mutton and it has darker flesh with a stronger flavour. Prime lamb is taken from five to seven month-old animals and it is known as spring lamb.

Look for firm, slightly pink meat with a fine-grained, velvety texture. The fat should be creamy white, firm and waxy.

Avoid meat that looks dry or dark and grainy, surrounded by yellow fat.

Storing

Lamb should be stored on a low shelf in the refrigerator, well away from other foods, in a covered dish large enough to contain any drips. Leave pre-packed meat in its packaging and use by the date given on the packet. When buying loose meat, chops and steaks should keep for two to four days, larger joints for up to five days. Use minced (ground) lamb on the day of purchase.

Lamb freezes well. Wrap it in freezer bags and seal tightly. Store small cuts in the freezer for up to three months, larger cuts for up to six months. Thaw overnight in a dish in the refrigerator.

THE BASIC CUTS OF LAMB

Prime cuts are taken from the top of the lamb carcass, along the middle of the back. They are from the muscle least used during the life of the animal and yield the most tender meat. These are the cuts to cook quickly, by grilling (broiling) and frying as well as roasting; these cuts can also be cooked slowly by moist methods, such as stewing and braising.

Cuts from the neck and lower legs, parts that worked hardest when the animal was alive, are cheaper, and they need slower, gentle cooking in a casserole or stew until tender.

Côte d'agneau is the French term for a loin or rack, also sometimes called best end of neck chop.

Below: Saddle of lamb, or double loin, is a huge roasting joint taken from both sides of the carcass.

Above: Chump chops are good for pan-frying and grilling.

Noisettes

Boned and rolled loin, tied, then sliced into small rounds, noisettes are good to pan-fry, sauté, griddle or grill (broil).

Double loin chops

Sometimes called Barnsley chops or butterfly chops, these are cut from a saddle of lamb. They are suitable for grilling, frying or braising.

Chump chops

An English cut, these chops are from between the leg and the loin, and they have a small round bone in the middle.

Saddle

This large roasting joint is the whole loin taken from both sides of the carcass and is sometimes called a double loin of lamb.

Leg

A tender cut, often divided into fillet and shank, which is sold both on the bone or boned.

Below: Roast or barbecue tender leg and leg steaks.

Loin

Usually sold as a joint, sometimes boned, stuffed and rolled, this prime cut is good for roasting. Loin chops can be cooked on a barbecue, griddled, grilled or pan-fried. Loin chops have a small T-bone (part of the backbone).

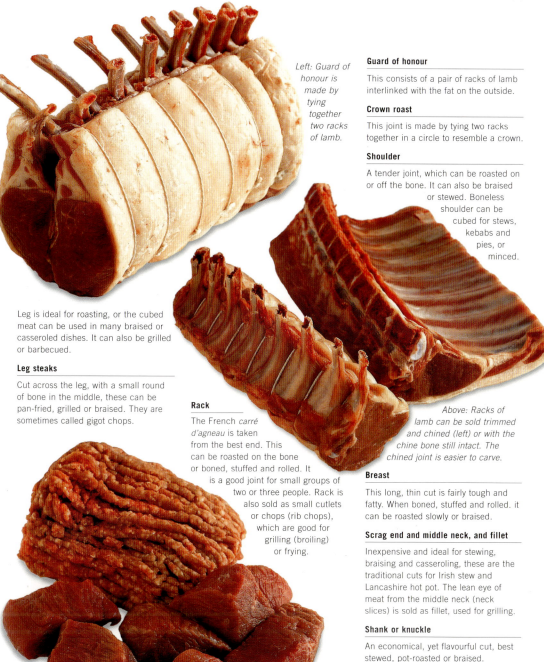

Left: Guard of honour is made by tying together two racts of lamb.

Guard of honour

This consists of a pair of racks of lamb interlinked with the fat on the outside.

Crown roast

This joint is made by tying two racks together in a circle to resemble a crown.

Shoulder

A tender joint, which can be roasted on or off the bone. It can also be braised or stewed. Boneless shoulder can be cubed for stews, kebabs and pies, or minced.

Leg is ideal for roasting, or the cubed meat can be used in many braised or casseroled dishes. It can also be grilled or barbecued.

Leg steaks

Cut across the leg, with a small round of bone in the middle, these can be pan-fried, grilled or braised. They are sometimes called gigot chops.

Rack

The French *carré d'agneau* is taken from the best end. This can be roasted on the bone or boned, stuffed and rolled. It is a good joint for small groups of two or three people. Rack is also sold as small cutlets or chops (rib chops), which are good for grilling (broiling) or frying.

Above: Racks of lamb can be sold trimmed and chined (left) or with the chine bone still intact. The chined joint is easier to carve.

Breast

This long, thin cut is fairly tough and fatty. When boned, stuffed and rolled. it can be roasted slowly or braised.

Scrag end and middle neck, and fillet

Inexpensive and ideal for stewing, braising and casseroling, these are the traditional cuts for Irish stew and Lancashire hot pot. The lean eye of meat from the middle neck (neck slices) is sold as fillet, used for grilling.

Shank or knuckle

An economical, yet flavourful cut, best stewed, pot-roasted or braised.

Minced or cubed lamb

Quick and easy, minced (ground) or cubed lamb are good in pies or kebabs.

Left: Minced and diced lamb

PREPARING LAMB

Boning a shoulder

Removing the blade and shoulder bones from a shoulder of lamb means that the joint can be rolled and tied or stuffed (see below right). Boning the joint means that it is much easier to carve uniform slices of meat.

1 Using a sharp knife, carefully scrape back the flesh to reveal the wide end of the blade bone.

2 When the edge of the bone is free, follow the shape of the blade to cut the meat carefully off the bone. Do this on both sides of the large, flat bone.

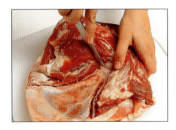

3 Cut right through the ball and socket joint to separate the blade and shoulder bones.

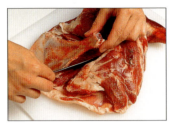

4 Hold the joint open, then pull the blade bone away from the meat, scraping off any meat from the narrow end of the bone (reserve this to include in stuffing, see below).

5 Cut and scrape the meat away from the shoulder bone and then pull the bone free. The joint is now ready to be stuffed and rolled or just rolled.

Stuffing a boned shoulder

1 Finely chop any meat trimmings left over from boning the shoulder. Mix with 30ml/2 tbsp chopped fresh herbs (any Mediterranean herbs work well – try a combination of rosemary, thyme, oregano and basil), 2 crushed garlic cloves, 1 finely chopped shallot, 115g/4oz fresh white breadcrumbs, and then season with plenty of salt and freshly ground black pepper.

2 Open out the boned shoulder and spread the stuffing evenly over it, leaving a space all around the edges of the meat. Carefully fold the meat back into its original shape, ensuring that all of the stuffing stays in place, or alternatively, roll the meat. Tie the joint neatly with string to keep the stuffing in place and to keep the joint in shape during cooking.

Boning a leg

Removing the bone before roasting makes space for stuffing the leg, if required (see below left for a simple stuffing), and the roast joint is easier to carve than a joint with the bone in.

1 Using a sharp knife, carefully trim off all the excess fat from the outside of the joint and carefully cut through the tendons at the bottom of the shank.

2 Cut around the pelvic bone and through the tendons, then remove the pelvic bone.

3 Carefully scrape the flesh away from the shank bone using a small, sharp knife (reserve any meat trimmings to include in stuffing), then cut through the tendons on the leg joint and pull out the shank bone.

Preparing crown roast

4 Cut around the leg bone, then twist and remove it.

Preparing a butterfly leg

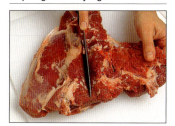

When the bones have been removed from the leg, cut the meat lengthways and open out the joint. When boning a leg for a butterfly finish, the meat can be cut down its length to remove the bones; this is easier than twisting them out. Open out the meat flat. The meat can be stuffed and rolled, or metal skewers can be inserted widthways to keep it flat, which is useful when cooking the whole leg on a barbecue.

Preparing rack of lamb

The best end of neck, or rack, come from one side of the rib cage. There are usually 6–9 cutlets (rib chops).

1 Cut off the skin and most of the fat.

2 If the rack isn't "chined", place the rack on its side and cut off the chine bone (the back bone).

3 Cut the fat off the ribs down the top 5cm/2in from the bone ends. Turn the joint over and score between the bones.

4 Cut and scrape away the meat and connective tissue between the bones.

Flavouring rack of lamb

A rack of lamb can be flavoured before roasting. First, sear the fat on the joint. Heat a little oil in a large frying pan and press the joint, fat side down, in the hot oil until browned, then remove from the pan and leave to cool. Spread the fat with 15ml/1 tbsp Dijon mustard. Press a mixture of chopped fresh herbs, ground spices and dried breadcrumbs into the mustard with your fingers.

Preparing crown roast

1 Prepare 2 racks of lamb as described left, then carefully cut the tissue that is between each rib so that the rack can be bent into position.

2 Stand the rack and carefully bend it into a semicircle, with the meat outside, to form the shape of one side of the crown. Push the ribs outwards at the top so that the crown will sit up straight.

3 Bend the second rack into shape and then tie string around the crown at 2.5cm/1in intervals to hold the racks together and in shape.

4 The crown of lamb is now ready for roasting. However, if you prefer, the central cavity of the crown of lamb can be stuffed (see the garlic and herb stuffing recipe, left) before roasting.

Preparing guard of honour

This consists of a pair of racks of lamb interlocked like soldiers' swords in a military guard of honour.

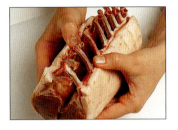

Prepare 2 racks of lamb. Hold 1 rack in each hand and push the racks together, interlocking the bones. Tie the racks at regular intervals to secure.

Cutting noisettes

Noisettes are thick slices of the boned and rolled loin. They can be pan-fried, chargrilled or griddled.

1 Trim off the thin fatty edge of the flap along the side of the boned loin, then tie the meat into a cylinder shape at 3.5cm/1¼in intervals.

2 Cut the loin into thick slices between the string. Flatten each noisette slightly.

Trimming and cutting fillet

The fillet is cut from the middle of the neck of lamb. It is a lean and tender cut that is well marbled with internal fat and it can be cut into medallions or cubes.

1 Trim off the thin membrane and any large areas of fat on the fillet.

2 To make medallions of lamb, cut the fillet into thin slices of an even width. Medallions can be either pan-fried or braised, then served in a sauce (see pan-frying, right).

3 To cut the fillet into cubes, first cut the meat lengthways into thick strips using a sharp knife, then cut the strips across into cubes. These tender cubes of lamb are ideal for marinating and making into kebabs (see making kebabs, right).

Marinating

This adds flavour and helps to keep the meat moist during cooking. Marinating overnight is best as this allows time for the flavours to develop fully and penetrate the meat. When time is short, marinating for 1–2 hours will still make all the difference to the taste.

1 Mix together the ingredients for the marinade in a dish that is large enough to hold the meat in a single layer. Do not use uncoated metal as this reacts with acids, such as vinegar, or plastic containers, which pick up the flavour of strong ingredients, such as garlic. A glass dish or bowl is ideal.

2 Add the meat to the marinade in the dish and turn it a few times to coat both sides thoroughly.

3 Cover the dish with clear film (plastic wrap) and leave the meat to marinate in a cool place or the refrigerator, turning the meat once or twice.

COOK'S TIP
Always remove lamb from the refrigerator about an hour before cooking and let it warm to room temperature. This improves the flavour of the meat and makes it more tender.

COOKING LAMB

Pan-frying

This is the traditional method for cooking lamb steaks, cutlets or chops. It is also a useful method for medallions.

Preheat the pan thoroughly, then grease it lightly with a little oil before adding the meat. Medallions are tender and cook quickly, so as soon as they are browned (2–3 minutes), turn and cook the second sides. When the medallions are cooked, transfer them to warmed plates and stir double (heavy) cream into the cooking juices with a sprinkling of fresh thyme leaves, salt and pepper. Heat until boiling to make a delicious, rich sauce. Spoon it over the cooked lamb, serve at once.

Griddling noisettes

Noisettes cook evenly and quickly, and many people prefer them to meat on the bone. The cooking time depends on the thickness of the noisettes: ensure they are all evenly thick so that they cook in the same length of time.

Heat a ridged griddle until hot, then add a little oil or butter. When the oil is hot or the butter foaming, add the noisettes and cook for 4–5 minutes on each side.

Grilling

This is a quick, easy and healthy way of cooking lamb cutlets or chops, allowing the fat to drip away during cooking. The high heat seals the meat quickly to lock in the juices and give a succulent result. Sprigs of rosemary can be inserted into the meat before cooking to add a delicious flavour to the cutlets or chops.

1 Trim off any excess fat around the cutlets or chops with a sharp cook's knife. Season well with salt and pepper.

2 Make a slit through the fat into the flesh and insert a sprig of rosemary. Preheat the grill (broiler) to high.

3 Place the cutlets on a lightly oiled grill rack and cook under a hot grill. Allow 4–6 minutes on each side; turning halfway through cooking.

Making kebabs

Use metal skewers or soak bamboo skewers in water for 30 minutes before threading the meat on them. Soaking wooden skewers helps to prevent them from burning during cooking.

1 Cut boneless leg, shoulder or neck fillet into 3.5cm/1¼in cubes.

2 Marinate the lamb, then drain the lamb and thread on to oiled skewers, alternating with vegetables. Leave a little space between each piece to ensure they cook evenly. Place the kebabs on an oiled rack over a preheated barbecue or under a very hot grill and cook, turning them frequently, for 6–8 minutes.

All about kebabs

The word kebab comes from the Arabic and means "on a skewer". Lamb makes excellent kebabs because it is lean and tender, and cooks very quickly.

Shish kebab, which means "meat on a skewer", was first eaten by Turkish soldiers who cooked chunks of lamb on their swords over open fires. Chunks of lamb are skewered with vegetables and grilled over charcoal.

Doner kebab consists of a whole leg of lamb, boned, marinated and roasted on a rotating vertical spit. It is often made with lamb that has been ground and then compressed into the shape of a leg of lamb. Slices are cut off and served with salad in pitta bread.

Barbecuing

Heat the barbecue about 30 minutes in advance, until the coals are ashen and very hot. Chops, leg steaks, cutlets and noisettes are all suitable.

Brush the meat with a little oil before placing on the barbecue. Cook for about 3 minutes on each side.

Stewing

Scrag end and middle neck (neck slices) are suitable cuts for stewing. Lamb on the bone can be layered in a casserole with sliced onions, bay leaves and other herbs, then water, stock or wine can be poured in to cover the meat. Season, then cook from a cold start for 2–3 hours at a low temperature, for a succulent, well-flavoured result.

Alternatively, the meat can be browned first. This is the best method for stews made with cubed lamb; it is also good for cooking lamb on the bone.

1 Brown the meat in a frying pan, then transfer to a flameproof casserole. Fry a chopped onion in the fat remaining in the pan, add stock, water or wine and bring to the boil, scraping all the residue off the pan. Pour this liquid over the lamb in the casserole. Add any chopped herbs or bay leaves.

2 Cover, then simmer gently for about 2½ hours or until very tender.

Braising

Leg steaks or chops are an excellent choice for braising on a bed of root vegetables. Prepare the vegetables, such as carrots, parsnips and onions, cutting them into chunks, then place them in a large flameproof casserole.

1 Heat a little oil in a frying pan; brown the lamb quickly on both sides.

2 Lay the lamb on top of the vegetables. Add stock to the frying pan used for browning the meat and bring to the boil, stirring to mix in all the sediment. Pour the stock over the lamb – it should cover the vegetables and part-cover the meat. Cover and simmer gently for 45–60 minutes.

Pot-roasting lamb shanks

Lamb shanks are tender and delicious when pot-roasted in the oven or on the hob (stovetop), on a bed of chopped aromatic vegetables moistened with a little red wine or well-flavoured stock, in a covered casserole.

1 Heat a large, heavy frying pan and add a little sunflower or olive oil. When the oil is hot, add the lamb shanks, in batches if necessary, and fry them over a high heat, turning them occasionally using tongs, until they are well browned on all sides.

2 Meanwhile, prepare a bed of thickly sliced or roughly diced vegetables, such as carrots, swede (rutabaga), leeks and onions, layered with sprigs of fresh thyme, bay leaves, rosemary, marjoram, or other aromatic herbs in a large, deep, flameproof casserole.

3 Place the lamb shanks on top of the vegetables and pour in enough robust red wine or stock just partially to cover the vegetables. Cover the casserole with a tight-fitting lid or foil and cook in a preheated oven at 180°C/350°F/Gas 4 for 1–1½ hours, until the lamb is very tender. Check halfway through cooking and add more liquid if necessary.

Roasting

Lamb is often served rare or medium rare. A meat thermometer is useful for checking the internal temperature of the meat. Insert it into the middle of the thickest part of the joint.

Roasting times for lamb
For rare lamb
Weigh the joint, then roast in a oven preheated to 230°C/450°F/Gas 8 for 10 minutes. Reduce the oven temperature to 180°C/350°F/Gas 4, and cook the lamb for the remaining time, allowing 18 minutes per 450g/1lb. The internal temperature of the joint should be 60°C/140°F.
For a medium result
Roast at 230°C/450°F/Gas 8 for 10 minutes, then at 180°C/350°F/Gas 4 for a further 25 minutes per 450g/1lb, plus 25 minutes. The internal temperature should be 70°C/158°F.
For well-cooked lamb
Roast at 230°C/450°F/Gas 8 for 10 minutes, then at 180°C/350°F/Gas 4 for a further 30 minutes per 450g/1lb, plus 30 minutes. The internal temperature should be 80°C/176°F.

1 Weigh the joint. Cut small, deep, slits all over the meat using the point of a small, sharp knife. Insert thin slivers of peeled garlic and small fresh rosemary or thyme sprigs into the slits.

2 Lay the leg of lamb in a roasting pan, fat-side up, and sprinkle with salt. Roast for the times given above.

3 Cover the cooked meat loosely with foil and leave to stand in a warm place for 10 minutes before carving. This standing time allows the meat to relax and the internal temperature to even out, making the meat easier to carve.

Carving leg of lamb

1 Start by cutting a wedge of meat from the top of the leg, near the thin end of the leg, but not right at the end. Cut down through the thick part of the meat as far as the bone.

2 Holding the joint firmly at the leg end, carve slices following the first cut made by the wedge; these are the prime slices of meat.

3 Turn the joint over and cut small slices down across the grain to remove the remaining meat.

Carving rack of lamb

Cut between the rib bones and serve the roast rack as cutlets (chops). This method is also used for crown roast and guard of honour; scoop out any stuffing with a spoon before cutting between the cutlets. Remove string from a crown roast before carving.

Wines to serve with lamb
Smooth, medium-bodied red wines best complement lamb. A good Margaux or St Emilion from Bordeaux goes down very well with roast lamb. As a less expensive alternative, try a Minervois, Fitou or Côtes du Roussillon from the south of France.

New Zealand is famous for its lamb and a Cabernet Sauvignon or Merlot from Hawkes Bay will complement most lamb dishes.

The Middle East is also sheep country and some of the better red wines from the Lebanon go down very well with lamb. Most of the country's vineyards are on the sides of the Bekaa Valley and they yield excellent fruity red wine from Cabernet Sauvignon, Carignan, Syrah and Grenache grapes.

It is also worth sampling some of the softer Napa Valley reds from California, or a medium-bodied Chianti from Italy with lamb chops. Unoaked Chilean Merlot goes well with moussaka and a fruity Australian Shiraz will make the most of lamb with mint sauce. Pour a lightly oaked Spanish Rioja to turn shepherd's pie into a real treat.

PORK, BACON, GAMMON AND HAM

You can use more or less every part of a pig for cooking. It is comparatively inexpensive, very versatile, generally tender and has an excellent flavour. However, pork, bacon, gammon (cured ham) and ham are not universally acceptable, and Jews and Muslims do not eat it. There are many theories as to why the meat of the pig is considered to be unclean, apart from the religious origins of the ban. Perhaps it is because of the mucky circumstances in which pigs are often reared; their proximity to man in some countries and the dangers of infection from eating the meat less than well-cooked; or the poor keeping qualities of pork in hot climates.

PORK

The pig has long been an important source of food in other communities throughout Europe, Asia and South and Central America. Pigs are inexpensive and easy to look after. They will eat anything and, unlike sheep and cattle, do not need a large area of land to graze. Until less than 50 years ago, pigs were reared in suburban backyards, fattened on kitchen leftovers and killed by the local butcher.

From ears to trotters (feet), virtually every part can be eaten, including the skin (but excluding a few internal organs, such as the spleen). Whole roasted suckling pig, highly seasoned brawns and meat pastes, stuffed and

Free-range pork

While cattle and sheep spend most of their lives outside, eating grass and moving freely around fields, some pigs are housed in buildings where light and temperature are strictly controlled. With increasing consumer awareness and demand for food with flavour, farmers are now reverting to more traditional and often organic methods of rearing pigs. Free-range pork and its products might cost more, but they have a far superior taste and come from pigs reared under humane conditions.

roasted joints, crisp-fried sweet-and-sour pork, and rich pork simmered in milk are a few examples to highlight the vast range of methods of cooking and serving pork. As for other meats, there are prime roasts and cuts that grill (broil) well; unlike other meats, the carcass does not yield very tough cuts. With trimming to remove sinews and excess fat, most of the meat is tender.

Pork is widely used in Chinese and Asian dishes, so much so that in Chinese cooking it is referred to as "meat" rather than by type. In both Chinese and Western cooking, the crisp, roasted skin is a delicacy. In Eastern European cooking, pork is excellent combined with cabbage or sauerkraut and fruits; it is also popular with dried beans and pulses in European and American dishes. Fresh pork was traditionally a food for late autumn, when pigs were fattened through the summer and killed in the cooler weather, ready for winter. Meat that could not be used fresh was cured for long keeping, providing bacon and ham.

The farmed pig is a descendant of wild boars that once roamed the woods and forests of Europe and Asia. There are two basic breeds, the long-backed Chinese pig and the heavier European or Danish pig. Pigs farmed today are well removed from the shorter, fatter and rounder animals that yielded fatty meat – they are longer, leaner and their carcasses contain a larger proportion of lean, prime cuts. They are reared primarily for curing and to supply the bacon market.

This process of selective breeding started in 1760 when Robert Bakewell, a Leicestershire farmer, crossed a Chinese pig with a European pig for the first time. The cosmetic Chinese features were bred out quite quickly, but the plumpness and the sweetness stayed behind. Traditionally, the pig's diet was adapted according to the ultimate use for which its meat was required, ensuring that the texture and flavour of the meat was the best, for example for certain cured hams. Specialist farmers still rear to these standards and old-fashioned breeds are

Above: The meat of pigs is considered unclean by some religions – this could relate to the pigs' living conditions.

again of great interest. Apart from specialist suppliers and high-quality pork products, some supermarkets also stock sausages labelled with the breed of pig from which the meat they contain was taken.

Buying

Look for firm, pale-pink flesh, which is moist but not damp or oily. The fat should be white, and the bones should be tinged with red. The skin should be dry and silky, not slimy or damp. Most pigs are slaughtered at around six months, when they yield meat with a fine texture. Coarse flesh and hard, white bones indicate that the animal is older and the meat less tender.

Storing

To avoid cross-contamination by meat juices, which may drip on to food that is to be eaten uncooked, store pork on a low shelf in the refrigerator, well away from and below cooked food and food that is to be eaten raw. Ideally, the meat should be placed on a rack in a dish and covered with a lid so that moisture can be retained while air can circulate freely. Pre-packed meat is best kept in its packaging as long as this is sealed and undamaged.

Always check and observe the use-by dates on packaged meats. As a guide when buying loose meat, minced (ground) pork will keep in the refrigerator for one to two days; pork cuts and joints for three to four days. It can be frozen for four to six months.

Nutrition

Pork was once thought of as a very fatty meat; however, modern breeding, rearing and butchering has resulted in pork becoming one of the lowest-fat meats available. The fat it does contain is also less saturated than the fat in other meats. Pork is a high-quality protein food, a good source of iron, zinc and B vitamins. It also provides many other trace elements, including copper, manganese and selenium.

BACON, GAMMON AND HAM

Originally, bacon was meat taken only from the back or side of a pig. Today it means cured meat taken usually, but not exclusively, from the back and sides of the pig. Gammon, which is the same joint as ham but milder in flavour, comes from the hind leg and is left attached to the side during curing and cut from it afterwards. Bacon is available as joints and chops as well as different types of rashers (strips).

Below: More and more pigs are being reared outdoors in units such as this one in Norfolk, England.

In Anglo-Saxon English, ham was the term for the part of the leg at the back of the knee (hence hamstring). It later came to refer to the thigh in general and in the 17th century began to mean the thigh of an animal that had been dried, salted and usually smoked. It was, typically, a pig's thigh, but mutton hams, venison hams and even bear hams were enjoyed in the 18th and 19th centuries.

In Britain and America, ham now refers to cured pig meat. It is most widely used for the cooked or ready-to-eat product or for dry-cured hams that can be eaten raw as well as cooked. Gammon steaks and cured and pressed pork shoulder are sometimes referred to as ham, especially in the USA.

Curing methods

There are three curing methods for bacon and gammon: dry coarse salt, brine or a mixture of salt, sugar, seasonings and preservatives. After salting, the meat may be smoked.

Every region and country has its own traditional method and recipe for curing ham, first in dry salt or brine and then sometimes smoked over a hardwood fire. The brine can be varied by the addition of sugar or molasses, herbs, spices or berries. Finally, the ham is left to dry and mature. The temperature and humidity during the drying, or smoking and drying, can be varied to produce different results. The geographical differences are still evident in the names of the hams that are available today: Parma ham from Parma in Italy; Virginia ham from the southern states of America; and York ham, Cumberland ham, Wiltshire ham and Suffolk ham from different regions of England.

Some dry-cured, smoked hams are eaten raw. Italian prosciutto is probably the most famous of these. In France, Bayonne ham is the equivalent, and German Westphalian ham is eaten uncooked. These are all sliced very finely before serving. They are also cooked for use in some dishes.

The hind legs and the loin make the best cured pork and ham.

Buying

Good-quality bacon has clear, pink, moist, but not wet, meat with an even layer of creamy-white fat.

When buying uncooked ham, such as prosciutto, look for deep-pink flesh and creamy-white fat. The ham should be moist, but not damp and should lie flat, not dry and curled at the edges. Unless pre-packed, it should be freshly sliced for you when you buy it. Look for a supplier who is competent at cutting large, paper-thin slices. The rind and some of the fat should be trimmed off before it is sliced. Reject broken slices and those that have been reduced to shreds, or slices that are too thick to be palatable when served raw.

Storing

Observe the use-by date on pre-packed bacon. Leave the bacon in its pack, then, when it is opened, store any leftovers wrapped in clear film (plastic wrap). Follow the storage instructions on the packet. If you buy good-quality loose bacon, wrap it in greaseproof (waxed) paper and a plastic bag. It will keep fresh for up to three weeks in the refrigerator. Keep the bacon in the coolest part of the refrigerator.

Store ham in the refrigerator. Leave pre-packed meat in its wrapping and use by the recommended date. Wrap slices of loose ham in waxed paper or greaseproof paper and clear film.

Bacon and ham do not freeze well as the salt used in curing promotes rancidity once they are frozen. Vacuum-packed bacon and ham have a slightly improved freezer life. The storage time depends on the curing process. As a general rule, it is not worth freezing high-quality bacon and ham cured by traditional methods as they keep for only two to three weeks and tend to be inferior when thawed. However, meat cured by modern methods will keep for one month or in some cases manufacturers suggest a freezer life of up to three months. This short freezing time also applies to dishes containing bacon – they will keep for up to four weeks. The bacon becomes rancid on longer storage and taints the dish.

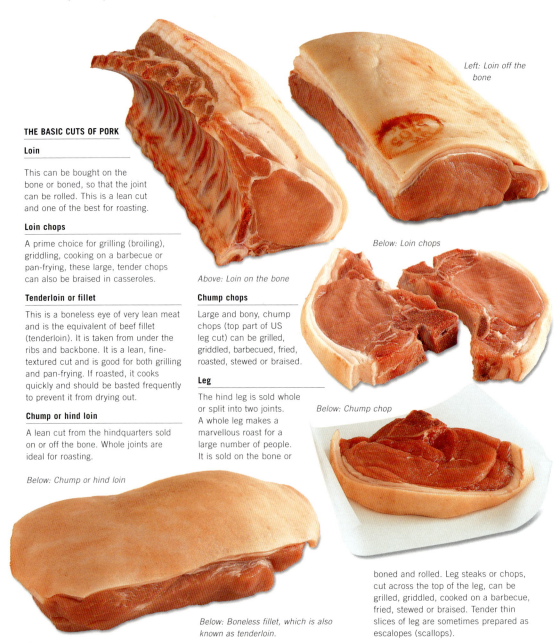

Left: Loin off the bone

THE BASIC CUTS OF PORK

Loin

This can be bought on the bone or boned, so that the joint can be rolled. This is a lean cut and one of the best for roasting.

Loin chops

A prime choice for grilling (broiling), griddling, cooking on a barbecue or pan-frying, these large, tender chops can also be braised in casseroles.

Above: Loin on the bone

Tenderloin or fillet

This is a boneless eye of very lean meat and is the equivalent of beef fillet (tenderloin). It is taken from under the ribs and backbone. It is a lean, fine-textured cut and is good for both grilling and pan-frying. If roasted, it cooks quickly and should be basted frequently to prevent it from drying out.

Chump or hind loin

A lean cut from the hindquarters sold on or off the bone. Whole joints are ideal for roasting.

Below: Chump or hind loin

Below: Loin chops

Chump chops

Large and bony, chump chops (top part of US leg cut) can be grilled, griddled, barbecued, fried, roasted, stewed or braised.

Leg

The hind leg is sold whole or split into two joints. A whole leg makes a marvellous roast for a large number of people. It is sold on the bone or

Below: Chump chop

boned and rolled. Leg steaks or chops, cut across the top of the leg, can be grilled, griddled, cooked on a barbecue, fried, stewed or braised. Tender thin slices of leg are sometimes prepared as escalopes (scallops).

Below: Boneless fillet, which is also known as tenderloin.

Leg fillet

This is cut across the top of the leg, including the bone in the middle. It is tender and good for roasting.

*Below:
Leg steaks*

Knuckle

This joint, known as shank in the US, is cut from the lower part of the leg and provides succulent meat when roasted slowly; it also has plenty of crackling.

Spare rib and spare rib chops

Taken from the fore end of the animal and sold either whole as a spare rib joint or cut up into spare rib chops. Suitable for slow roasting, braising and grilling (broiling) or griddling.

Spare ribs

Chinese-style spare ribs are cut from the belly rather than from the neck end of the carcass, the area from which spare rib chops and joints are cut. They are best marinated, then grilled or cooked on a barbecue.

Above: The top end of a leg of pork on the bone is a large joint that makes an excellent roast.

Right: Chinese-style spare ribs are cut from the pig's belly and are best marinated for several hours, then grilled or cooked on a barbecue.

Left: Shoulder steaks are sold both with and without the bone, but either way they are delicious and succulent, and can be cooked in a number of ways, such as grilling and braising.

Shoulder or blade

Taken from the fore end and sold on or off the bone, this cut can be roasted or pot-roasted (if whole) but is mostly boned, trimmed of sinews and membranes, then cut into cubes for making stews, casseroles or kebabs.

Shoulder steaks

Marbled with fat, with or without the bone, these can be grilled, griddled, barbecued, fried, stewed or braised.

*Right:
Knuckle of
pork and
boneless leg
fillet are
good for
roasting.*

Below: Hand and spring

Hand and spring

From the fore end of the animal, this has quite a lot of sinew and connective membranes, but, when trimmed, the meat is tender and has an excellent flavour. Known as shoulder in the US, it is suitable for slow roasting or braising as a joint.

Above: Rolled belly of pork is a fatty joint that is delicious either slow roasted or pot-roasted.

Belly

Traditionally a fatty cut, but less so on the modern pork carcass, belly (side) can be rolled and tied to make a neat joint. It is also used for mincing (grinding) or making sausages. Belly of pork can be slow and pot-roasted, grilled (broiled), griddled, cooked on a barbecue or stewed.

THE BASIC CUTS OF BACON AND GAMMON

Bacon and bacon joints are cut from the fore quarter; ham and gammon (cured ham) from the hind quarter. Collar from the front of the carcass is sold as joints, for boiling, or as wide, fairly lean rashers (strips). These are economical, but not so tender as those from the middle of the carcass, described below. Joints from the fore quarter are sold as bacon joints and are ideal for boiling, giving a good flavour, or for dicing and stewing or adding to soups. Offcuts (scraps) from bacon and gammon are inexpensive and ideal for flavouring dishes.

Right: Gammon leg joints may be on or off the bone.

Middle gammon

Gammon is the cured leg and may be cooked on the bone or boned and rolled. Middle gammon is a prime cut taken from the wide part of the leg. It can be boiled or baked, or cooked by both methods.

Gammon slipper

A small joint, which is very lean, but not considered as good as the middle cut.

Gammon hock

This is a large joint, almost the whole gammon, but without the knuckle.

Gammon knuckle

The end of the gammon, this includes the bone. It is often used to flavour soups or for making stock, or it can be boned and rolled. This is a small joint for boiling or baking. It can also be cut into cubes for casseroles.

Gammon steaks

These are thick slices cut from the gammon joint.

Middle or through-cut bacon

This is the back and streaky bacon in one piece, which curves from the top of the carcass around under the belly (the streaky end).

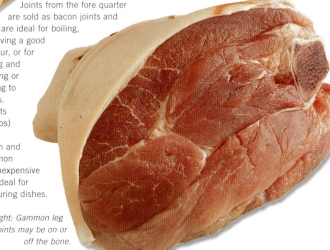

Above: Gammon steaks are cut from the boneless joint.

Above: Lean rashers of back bacon

Pancetta

This bacon is the Italian equivalent of streaky bacon and can be bought in strips or round slices cut from a roll. It is cured by traditional methods, and may be unsmoked or smoked.

Wines to serve with pork, gammon, ham and bacon

At its best, Beaujolais is deliciously light, heady and fruity. Examples include the smooth wines of Brouilly, Fleurie, Moulin-à-Vent and Saint Amour. These go well with pork, as do some of the reds from the south of France, such as Minervois, Fitou and Côtes du Roussillon.

While most people tend to drink soft, fruity reds with pork, others prefer light, rounded white wines, such as the buttery Chardonnays from the Hunter Valley in Australia. These go well with grilled pork chops, or gammon, bacon or ham. If you want to be a little more adventurous, try a medium sweet Kabinett from Germany. These wines are not particularly fashionable, but they can be very enjoyable with pork dishes, particularly those cooked in cream sauces. And, of course, cider goes extremely well with all pork and apple dishes.

Below: Middle bacon includes both streaky and back.

Back bacon

This lean cut comes from the back, along the top of the carcass. The width of the bacon rashers vary according to the position along the carcass and the size of the carcass. Bacon chops are thick slices of cured back pork – they can be grilled (broiled), griddled, cooked on a barbecue, baked, pan-fried and prepared like pork chops.

Streaky bacon

Traditionally very fatty, but less so now as modern techniques have produced pigs with a smaller amount of fat. This is the belly end of the through-cut or middle. It is best grilled, but can also be used for barding the breast portions of poultry and game birds.

Above: Streaky bacon

Above: Pancetta

THE BASIC TYPES OF HAM

There are many different types of ham. Some, like the famous Prosciutto di Parma from Italy, are intended to be eaten in their raw, cured state in paper-thin slices, others require further cooking, and many are sold pre-cooked. Factors that influence the flavour of hams include the breed of pig and its diet, and the curing process: whether the meat has been dry-salted and brined, the length of time that it has been cured and whether it has been air-dried or smoked (and if so whether over applewood, beechwood, hickory or oak). A wide variety of flavourings, such as treacle (molasses) and beer, may be added during the curing process.

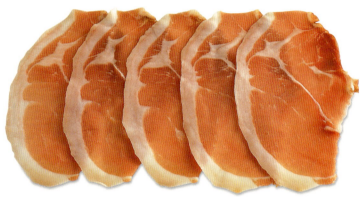

Above: Jambon d'Ardennes is a pale-pink, raw ham from Belgium

Above: Bayonne ham

Above: Iberico ham

Above: Serrano ham

Hams for Eating Raw

Bayonne ham Golden-coloured, French cured, smoked ham.

Iberico ham This exceptional raw, cured ham is made in south and west Spain. The hams come only from Iberian pigs.

Jambon d'Ardennes This is a pale-pink, raw, cured ham from Belgium. It can be very thinly sliced and eaten as is or sliced more thickly and then pan-fried.

Landrauch A dry, strongly flavoured, smoked ham from Germany.

Lachsschinken This pink, moist ham from Germany is made from smoked foreloin and is wrapped in a thin layer of creamy-white pork fat. The small, round slices are eaten raw.

Prosciutto crudo This is the Italian term for raw, cured ham; **Parma ham** or **prosciutto di Parma** is probably the most famous type. The ham comes from pigs fed on parsnips, and whey left over from making Parmesan cheese. It is dry-cured with salt, sugar and spices for at least nine months and sometimes up to two years. For part of this time it is weighted, which gives the ham its classic, flattened shape.

Serrano ham *Jamón serrano*, or "mountain ham", is a Spanish dry-salted, raw ham. The name was formerly used for all Spanish raw hams, but now refers to hams from white pigs reared in two regions of southern Spain.

Westphalian This is a German raw, cured and smoked ham. The pigs are fed on acorns and the ham is smoked over beech and juniper.

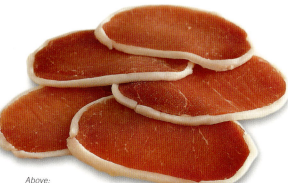

Above:
Lachsschinken, a German raw
ham often eaten with horseradish.

Right:
Prosciutto is perhaps the
most famous type of cured ham.

Cooked Hams

Bradenham ham This smoked, black-skinned ham from Chippenham in England has been made since 1781. The ham, which has a sweet flavour, is first dry-cured, then placed in a mixture of spices, brown sugar and molasses.

Brunswick ham This is a mild-flavoured ham from Germany.

Jambon de Paris/jambon blanc/jambon glacé These lightly salted, unsmoked French hams are usually bought cooked and sliced, and are eaten cold.

Kentucky ham An American dry-salted ham with a delicate flavour, which is smoked over corn cobs, and hickory and apple or sassafras wood. The pigs are fattened on acorns, beans, clover and grains, and the hams are left to mature for up to a year after salting.

Virginia ham A group of lean, smoked hams from the United States, of which **Smithfield ham** is considered the best. This ham comes from razor-back pigs raised outdoors in Virginia and North Carolina, where they feed on acorns, beechnuts and hickory nuts, before being fattened on peanuts and corn. The ham is cured by dry-salting with salt and pepper and is then smoked over hickory, apple and oak, and aged for a year. It can be served raw, but is usually boiled or baked, and can be eaten hot or cold.

York ham This is the name of a curing method rather than a type of ham, and the hams are now made in countries other than England. The ham is dry-salted and smoked, then matured for several months. **Green York ham** is also dry-cured. This delicately flavoured ham can be bought raw and needs to be cooked, either by boiling or baking (or both), or it can be bought ready cooked and sliced. It is eaten either hot or cold.

Right:
Bradenham
ham is a rich-
tasting English
ham flavoured
with spices.

Above: York
ham was originally only
produced in England, but it is now
made in countries all over the world.

PREPARING PORK

Trimming fillet

Lift the edge of the fatty membrane and carefully peel it away from the fillet (tenderloin). You can do this easily with your fingers, but it helps if you run the blade of a sharp knife down the underside of the membrane close to the meat to help separate it from the meat.

Cutting strips of fillet

Lay the trimmed fillet on a chopping board, with one of the narrow ends facing you. Use a long, sharp knife, to cut the meat lengthways into several 1–2cm/½–¾in wide strips.

Cutting cubes of fillet

Cut across the strips of trimmed fillet to make even-size cubes. These are ideal for kebabs.

Flattening fillet

1 Trim off all fat and remove the fatty membrane. Hold the top of the fillet and use a long, sharp knife to slice 4cm/1½in into the meat, this should be about halfway into it.

2 Lift the top slice and fold it back, as you carefully cut to within 1cm/½in of the opposite edge.

3 Lay the prepared fillet out on a large sheet of clear film (plastic wrap) and carefully fold back the top slice to open the meat to double its original width. Cover the fillet with a second sheet of clear film.

4 Use the flat side of a wooden mallet or a wooden rolling pin to beat out the fillet carefully and evenly to the required thickness for cooking.

Cutting medallions

1 Trim any fat and the thin membrane from the pork fillet, then, working from the thick end, cut off thick slices at a slight angle to make neat, round medallions of equal thickness.

2 Place the slices between sheets of clear film and gently beat flat using the flat side of a wooden mallet or a rolling pin. Beat to the required size and thickness for cooking.

Stuffing pork chops

Pork chops cut from the loin can be boned and stuffed before they are cooked, to add extra flavour. The chops can simply be slashed horizontally from the round, meat side, but they are especially good when trimmed and boned as shown below.

1 First trim off the fat from the chops. Use a sharp knife and work from the narrow end of the chop, carefully cutting away the rind with the band of fat. Next remove the bone from the chop. Cut the flesh along the line of the bone, keeping the knife as near as possible to it. Pull the bone away from the meat as you cut and twist the point of the knife to free the meat from the the corner of the bone.

2 Cut a shallow slit about 4cm/1½in long into the rounded side of the chop, halfway up its depth. Carefully press the knife blade deeper into the chop, but not right through to the other side, and cut backwards and forwards using the point of the knife blade to hollow out a deep, wide pocket almost to the edges of the meat.

3 Open up the pocket in the chop, and push in the stuffing using your fingers or a teaspoon. Press the stuffing and meat firmly to distribute the stuffing evenly throughout the cavity.

Stuffings for pork chops

Mix the ingredients and use these stuffings as they are for a light result. Combine the stuffing ingredients with fresh white breadcrumbs for a firmer mixture.
• Shredded rocket (arugula) with cored and diced eating apple. Peel the apple first, if you prefer.
• Chopped dried apricots, finely shredded spinach, chopped ham and chopped fresh parsley.
• Peeled and chopped roasted (bell) peppers with crushed garlic and finely chopped eating apples.

Boning and stuffing loin

This has two advantages: you can flavour the loin of pork with a tasty stuffing (see right for some suggested combinations) and the cooked meat is also far easier to carve.

1 Remove the skin and excess fat by cutting it off close to the meat using a large, sharp knife. Firmly pull and fold back the fat and skin as you remove them from the joint.

2 Hold the loin firmly in position on the board and cut between the ribs, taking care not to cut any further down into the meat than the thickness of the ribs.

3 Using a meat cleaver or large chef's knife, carefully cut down behind the ribs, keeping the blade as near to the bones as possible.

Stuffings for loin of pork
• Diced eating apple, chopped onion, fresh white breadcrumbs and a little white wine vinegar.
• Chopped bacon, raisins, fresh white breadcrumbs and parsley.

4 Work the blade down and around the chine bone, lifting the bones away from the meat as they are cut free.

5 Open out the loin and lay it flat, then cut two slits lengthways into the meat, taking care not to cut right through. Push the stuffing into the slits that have been cut along the joint.

6 Roll up the loin from one long side and tie securely with fine string in several places along its length.

COOKING PORK, BACON AND GAMMON

These are tender meats and most cuts can be roasted or baked, or cooked using other dry cooking methods. Hocks and trotters (feet) are the exceptions; they should be boiled to soften the connective tissue and release the small amount of well-flavoured meat they yield. Once boiled, hocks can be trimmed, stuffed and roasted. Some cuts, such as hand and spring (shoulder) have more sinews and are best slow roasted but, unlike beef, pork has no areas of tough muscle that need to be simmered to become tender.

Pan-frying

This is a traditional method for cooking chops, steaks and escalopes (scallops). Use a heavy, non-stick frying pan.

1 Dab a little sunflower oil on kitchen paper and use to grease the pan. Heat the pan until it is very hot (almost smoking). Add the meat and cook for about 3 minutes on each side.

2 Alternatively, pan-fry lean cuts in a mixture of butter and oil. Heat the oil in the pan before adding the butter. On its own, butter burns easily (unless it is clarified). Make sure the oil and butter are sizzling before adding the meat.

Stir-frying

This is a quick cooking method for thin, even strips or fine slices of pork. The majority of pork is suitable as long as all the sinew, membrane and fat are trimmed; prime cuts, such as fillet (tenderloin) or escalopes (scallops) are ideal. Most supermarkets sell pork ready cut into fine strips for stir-frying. Use a wok or a large, heavy frying pan.

1 Heat a little oil in the wok or pan until it is smoking hot.

2 Add the pork in batches and stir-fry over a high heat. Remove the cooked meat before adding a fresh batch. If you add too many strips at once, the temperature will drop and the meat will not cook quickly enough.

Griddling

This is another method of frying, in a ridged pan. A pan with a non-stick coating is best. The fat drains off the meat into the deep ridges and the meat is seared with a lined pattern.

1 Preheat the griddle until it is almost smoking. Brush the meat very lightly with a little oil. (Sunflower oil is very mild and does not change the flavour of the meat.)

2 Add the meat to the hot griddle. Don't overfill the pan.

3 Cook for 3 minutes on each side (a pair of tongs is useful for turning chops). At the end of cooking, if the fat is not well browned, use the tongs to hold the chops with the rim of fat on the griddle. Turn the fat to brown it along its length.

Grilling

This is a quick, easy and healthy way of cooking pork chops as it allows the fat to drip away during cooking. The intense heat of the grill (broiler) seals the meat quickly, keeping the juices in and giving succulent results.

1 Preheat the grill until very hot. Using a sharp cook's knife, carefully trim off any excess fat and gristle from around the chops.

2 Brush the chops with a little sunflower oil, then place the chops on an oiled rack under the grill.

3 Cook the chops for 3 minutes on each side, or until they are well browned and cooked through.

Apple sauce

This tart sauce is the traditional accompaniment for roast pork. Cooking apples give the sauce a delicious sweet-sour flavour, which cuts the richness of roast pork.

1 Peel, core and thickly slice 450g/1lb tart cooking apples. Place the apples in a small, heavy pan and add 75g/3oz/6 tbsp demerara (raw) sugar.

2 Heat gently, stirring occasionally, until the juice runs from the apples and the sugar dissolves. Continue to cook, stirring, until the apples are soft and pulpy.

3 Beat well, then spoon into a serving dish. Cover the surface of the sauce with clear film (plastic wrap) and serve cold.

Barbecuing

The coals must be lit 30 minutes in advance and be ashen in appearance, which is when they are extremely hot but not flaming. Distribute the coals evenly before starting to cook. The cooking rack must not be too near to the coals: the heat will be too fierce and the meat will dry out and become tough. If the rack is too far from the coals, the meat will not cook properly.

Marinating pork in a full-flavoured mixture for several hours or overnight gives the best results when barbecuing, especially with spare ribs or other cuts that are not from prime areas of the carcass. Spare ribs may be cooked in stock until tender, then drained, cooled and marinated before being finished on the barbecue – this is practical when cooking for a crowd when there may not be time to attend to the cooking, making sure the ribs are turned frequently and cooked evenly.

Roasting

1 Use a meat thermometer to check the internal temperature. Insert it into the thickest part of the meat, ensuring that it does not touch any bone. Pork is done when the internal temperature of the joint reaches 80°C/176°F.

2 Cover the joint with foil and set aside for 10 minutes. This allows the meat to settle and relax, so it is easier to carve.

Roasting times for pork
For well-cooked pork allow about 10 minutes at 230°C/450°F/Gas 8, then a further 30 minutes per 450g/1lb, plus an extra 30 minutes at 180°C/350°F/Gas 4.
For joints on the bone allow about 35 minutes per 450g/1lb, plus an extra 35 minutes for boned and rolled joints. Weigh stuffed joints after they have been stuffed.

Pot-roasting

Since most pork is tender, this method is used for cuts that tend to have more sinew, such as knuckle. Trotters (feet) can be pot-roasted or braised.

1 First heat a little sunflower oil in a flameproof casserole until very hot.

2 Add the meat and cook over a high heat, turning frequently, until browned on all sides. Add root vegetables and a little liquid, such as stock, wine or beer. Cover and cook on the hob (stovetop) or in the oven until the meat is tender.

Stewing, braising and casseroling

These are all long, slow, moist methods of cooking, which can be done in the oven or on the hob (stovetop). The meat is simmered gently in a flavourful liquid such as wine, water, beer or stock.

1 Trim off any excess fat and cut the meat into even-size cubes (about 2.5cm/1in).

2 The meat may be tossed in seasoned flour before cooking if a flour-thickened sauce is required. This gives a dark, rich result. Shake off any excess flour before browning the meat.

3 Heat 30ml/2 tbsp sunflower oil in a flameproof casserole. Add the meat in batches, a handful at a time, and cook over a high heat, turning frequently, until the meat is browned on all sides.

4 Use a slotted spoon to remove each batch of meat from the casserole, and allow the casserole to reheat before adding the next batch. Add a little more oil if necessary before adding the meat.

5 Add any flavouring vegetables, such as leeks, onions and carrots, to the casserole and cook in the remaining fat and juices, stirring occasionally, until softened and beginning to brown.

6 Return all the meat to the casserole and pour in the liquid. Bring to the boil, then simmer gently on the hob or transfer to a preheated oven and cook until the meat is tender. The casserole may be covered for the entire duration of the cooking time or it may be uncovered towards the end of the time to allow some of the cooking liquid to evaporate to thicken the sauce.

COOKING BACON OR GAMMON

If the gammon is cured by a traditional method, it may be salty and should be soaked in cold water to cover for 12 hours. However, most meat cured by modern methods is not too salty and it will be lacking in flavour if soaked. Check the information on the label or ask the butcher for details. As a guide, meats cured by traditional methods are generally available from specialist shops, high-quality butchers' or by mail order.

Boiling

Weigh the joint and calculate the cooking time at 20 minutes per 450g/1lb, plus 20 minutes.

1 Put the meat in a large casserole or pan with enough fresh cold water to cover. Bring the water to the boil and skim off the scum that rises to the surface. Simmer for 30 minutes. Drain the meat and discard the water.

2 Return the drained meat to the pan and cover with fresh cold water. Start cooking again, this time adding some flavouring ingredients, such as chopped apple or onion, cider, wine or cloves depending on how you are going to serve the meat, once it is cooked.

3 Cover the casserole and simmer the meat gently for the calculated time, beginning the timing at this stage.

Removing the rind, baking and glazing

While the meat is still hot the rind will come off easily, leaving a smooth surface on the fat.

1 Leave the meat to cool slightly in its cooking stock, then drain while still hot. Use a sharp knife to loosen the rind, then fold it back as you peel it off, cutting between it and the fat. This leaves an even layer of fat on the joint.

2 The fat can be finished with dried breadcrumbs or scored and studded with cloves if it is to be baked. Score deep lines across the fat, then score the fat in the opposite direction to mark out equal diamond shapes.

3 Stud the surface of the fat with whole cloves, placing 1 in the centre of each diamond of fat.

4 Sprinkle the meat generously with demerara (raw) sugar, pressing it lightly on to the fat. Bake in a preheated oven at 200°C/400°F/Gas 6 for about 20 minutes, basting regularly, until the sugar melts and browns, giving the fat an attractive sticky glaze. The meat can be thickly sliced and served hot, or left to cool completely before slicing and serving cold.

Alternative glazing mixtures
The following ingredients all work well as glazes for baked gammon as an alternative to a coating of sugar: try apple juice combined with clear honey; maple syrup; soy sauce mixed with light soft brown sugar and a little medium or dry sherry; or a tangy, orange marmalade mixed with a little clear honey to sweeten it. To ensure that the glaze gives a shiny, attractive appearance to the baked meat, baste the meat regularly during cooking with a little extra fresh glaze.

COOKING BACON

Bacon rashers (strips) can be grilled (broiled), griddled or fried. They are used in many ways in cooking, wrapped around ingredients to flavour them and prevent them from drying out during cooking or cut up and cooked with other foods as a flavouring ingredient. When cooking whole rashers, trim off any rind, then snip the fat at regular intervals to prevent the bacon from curling up and cooking unevenly.

Frying

This is the traditional way of cooking bacon. Grease a frying pan with a little oil on a pad of kitchen paper – there is no need to add more oil as the bacon will yield plenty of fat during cooking.

Heat the pan until hot. Lay the bacon rashers in the frying pan and fry over a medium-high heat for about 4–8 minutes, turning once.

Grilling

For a crispier result, bacon is best grilled. Preheat the grill (broiler). Lay the rashers on a rack and grill for 4–8 minutes, turning once. The fat drips away from the bacon as it cooks, so this is the better method when little fat is required with the meat.

SAUSAGES AND CURED MEATS

Fresh and cured sausages are meat mixtures, usually enclosed in casings. Originally sausages were made from all the offcuts from the carcass – offal (innards), fatty or tough scraps or irregular bits of meat. Mixed with herbs, spices, flavouring ingredients, salt and saltpetre for preservation, the meat was packed into lengths of intestine or other suitable organs, tied firmly and hung to dry and cure. These were not neat, uniformly cylindrical products even though they were, in effect, one of the earliest forms of convenience food. The casings often created sausages of different lengths, widths and shapes – haggis, the famous Scottish sausage of lamb offal packed in a sheep's stomach, is a good example.

Although casings were used for hanging and curing sausages intended for long-term storage, they were not essential. The mixture was sometimes pressed into shape, then coated with fat, flour or breadcrumbs. English faggots and French *crépinette* are both types of sausage, shaped into small balls, then wrapped in caul, the thin lacy covering of fat and membrane surrounding internal organs.

Sausages may have originated as a means of using up the remnants of the carcass after killing a pig and an essential way of preserving fresh meat, but they have moved on a long way since their humble origins.

Curing is an ancient method of preserving meat and meat products by salting and/or drying to prevent decay. Curing has long been used to preserve buffalo meat and beef. For example, *pemmican* is a

Below: Haggis

dried meat mixture, prepared by Native Americans. Dried buffalo, bison or venison is pounded with fat, seasonings and dried fruit, then packed into intestines or skins made from buffalo hide. In Mexico, sun-dried strips of buffalo meat were originally known as *charqui*, which later became jerk beef or jerky.

The three types of sausages

There are three kinds of sausage: fresh sausages; cured or dried sausages; and cooked sausages. Fresh sausages are raw and ready to cook – the British pork sausage is a good example. Cured or dried sausages are preserved sausages; salami is probably the best known of these. Cooked sausages include ones used for slicing, such as garlic sausage; or other types for spreading, such as liver sausage; plus other sausages that may be reheated or cooked again, for example frankfurters.

Nutrition

The nutritional value of sausages varies widely, not only according to the type of sausage, but also within the different groups, because every sausage contains different ingredients or varying proportions of the same ingredients. As a rule, sausages have a high fat content compared to lean meat, poultry or offal. Cured meats have a similar nutritional value to fresh meats.

FRESH SAUSAGES

The range of fresh sausages available varies according to food fashions and their popularity. There is an incredible choice, from coarse or

Above: Just a selection of British sausages, clockwise from top left: Beef and Guinness; pork; Lincolnshire, apple and pork chipolata sausages; venison; pork and beef; and Cumberland.

fine meat sausages made according to traditional recipes, to quite bizarre combinations of seasonings, fruit, nuts, vegetables and cheese added to basic meat mixtures. The selection changes according to the whim of the producer.

Classic ingredients

Fat in modest amounts is an important ingredient in traditional sausage fillings, bringing flavour and keeping the mixture moist. Fatty, flavourful cuts of pork, such as belly (side), are ideal for making sausages. Beef and veal are also used alone or combined with pork. Fresh bread is a traditional ingredient for binding the mixture; dried breadcrumbs and other cereals are inferior mainly because they are often added in large quantities when they absorb too much excess fat instead of allowing it to baste and flavour the meat before draining away. Inexpensive fillers are also used to make a wide range of economical sausages, often with a large amount of flavouring ingredients and artificial colouring agents added to compensate for the poor quality of the basic recipe.

Fresh or dried herbs are typical traditional seasonings, often combined with spices, such as mace, nutmeg, paprika and pepper. Garlic is another important flavouring ingredient for sausages, along with onions and leeks.

Casings and coatings

Intestines (also known as chitterlings) are the traditional casings for fresh sausages, but synthetic alternatives are widely used. Skinless sausages are also available and some firmer mixtures can be coated in flour or beaten egg and fresh or dried breadcrumbs.

Buying fresh sausages

When purchasing pre-packed products, always check the information on the ingredients they contain. Check the dates by which the pack should be sold and used. Whether packed or loose, look for sausages made with a large proportion of high-quality meat (at least 70 per cent) and natural seasonings or flavouring ingredients. Look at the texture, colour and plumpness of the sausage. Avoid products that are a strange, artificial colour compared to the ingredients they contain.

Fresh sausages should look plump and well filled, but not so full that they look fit to burst. They should look moist

Right: Italian sausages, clockwise from left: salsiccie casalinga, the large cotechino, luganeghe and salmelle.

and fresh. Reject sausages with dried patches or ends, discoloured areas or those that are wet, slimy or weeping. Smell is a good indicator of freshness and it is unwise to buy from a shop that smells unpleasant.

Storing fresh sausages

Leave pre-packed sausages in their wrapper and store in the coldest area of the refrigerator. Use within the date given on the packet. Transfer loose sausages to a suitable dish and cover with clear film (plastic wrap) or a lid, then use within two days. Keep highly aromatic sausages sealed otherwise they are likely to taint other foods.

Many types of fresh sausage freeze well, but this depends entirely on the ingredients they contain. Sausages highly flavoured with garlic should be at least double wrapped, otherwise they will taint other foods in the freezer.

TYPES OF FRESH SAUSAGE

Britain is famous for its fresh sausages: pork and beef are the main types, but chicken, venison and game sausages are all available. Italy, France

Left: German sausages include, clockwise from top right, frankfurters, Bratwurst, Bockwurst and Knoblauchwurst.

and Germany all have their own specialities, but these countries are particularly known for their cured sausages. The following is an overview of international fresh sausages.

Andouillette and the larger andouille These are made with pork, chitterlings, pepper, wine and onions and are sometimes smoked.

Bockwurst A smoked, German sausage that looks like a large frankfurter.

Bordeaux sausage This is a fairly small sausage that is highly seasoned.

Bratwurst A pale, fine-textured German sausage for frying. Made with pork or veal and seasoned with a combination of salt, pepper and mace.

Chipolata sausage Slim, fine-textured British pork sausage, traditionally high quality and a breakfast favourite. Skinless versions are produced, but do not compare well with the traditional sausage. A long length of chipolatas is known as a string of sausages.

Cotechino A coarse pork sausage flavoured with white wine and spices.

Cumberland sausage A coarse-textured British pork sausage seasoned with pepper. It is traditionally very long and is usually curled and cooked in a round.

Lincolnshire sausage British pork sausage flavoured with sage and thyme.

Luganeghe A thin pork sausage popular in northern Italy.

Merguez Spicy Algerian sausage made of beef and mutton and flavoured with red (bell) pepper.

Above: Toulouse sausages are flavoured with herbs and garlic.

CURED AND SMOKED SAUSAGES

There are literally thousands of cured and smoked sausages and, between the supermarkets and independent delicatessens in larger towns and cities, the choice can be quite overwhelming.

Left: Try to buy cured sausages, such as this Toscana, freshly sliced. Avoid ready-sliced sausages that look off-colour or dry around the edges.

Oxford sausage British sausage made from pork and veal.

Salchichas Small Spanish fresh sausage made with pork.

Salsiccie These Italian fresh sausages are bought ready for cooking. They are made according to local recipes, of which there are many types.

Salsiccie casalinga Meaning "home-made sausage", this is a rustic Italian sausage usually made with pure pork.

Saveloy English smoked sausage made from pork and beef; it also contains lights and a little saltpetre, which gives it a reddish hue.

Thick link sausages The standard British sausage, sometimes referred to as "links". There are traditional regional recipes made with pork or beef or a mixture of the two, as well as a huge range of contemporary flavours.

Toulouse sausage This is a chubby, coarse pork sausage, which is herby, highly seasoned and flavoured with garlic.

Preserving methods

There are many different methods of curing or smoking, many still based largely on traditional principles of preservation. Salt and saltpetre (potassium nitrate) are used to preserve the meat, while spices and herbs are used for flavouring. A wide variety of other ingredients can be added for flavour, including vegetables, wine and spirits. Sugar or other sweetening may be added, particularly when the salt is used in the form of a brine rather than as a dry cure.

Above: Fuet is a thin, firm-textured Spanish cured sausage that is bought whole to slice at home.

Left: Spanish chorizo and long, thin salchichas

For cured or dried sausages, the mixture is packed into the casing and then hung in an airy environment (usually cool, but sometimes hot) until dried. The middle of the sausage mixture dries more slowly than the outside and it ferments slightly. This is all part of the curing process, giving many salamis and cured sausages their slightly tangy flavour.

Smoking is an additional, traditional method of drying and imparting flavour to the cured sausages or meat. This process is carefully controlled, with specific types of wood, such as hickory, beech, juniper or oak, being used to give the sausages or cured meats their individual flavours. Sausages and meats may be lightly or heavily smoked.

Left: Felinetti is a delicately flavoured Italian salami.

Below: Milanese salami

Left: Napoli salami

Buying cured sausages and meats

There is such a wide range that it is difficult to make general comments. Cured sausages and cured and cooked meats must be fresh. Avoid products that are dull or dried-out and off-colour. The cured or cooked meats or sausages should be freshly sliced for you; many supermarkets and delicatessens slice popular products in advance to save time, but check that the slices have been cut fairly recently. Meats that have been sliced for many hours will look dry, especially around the edges: reject these. Pre-packed products vary greatly in quality and it is usually easy to assess them by appearance and also by price.

Below: Kuelbasa, a strongly flavoured Polish, smooth garlic sausage

Storing cured sausages and meats

The old-fashioned pantry is the ideal place for hanging whole cured meats or sausages. The refrigerator is the practical option for modest amounts and today's household. Leave pre-packed products in their sealed wrapping. Transfer loose, sliced meats to a plate and cover with clear film (plastic wrap) or wrap them closely in waxed paper, folding the edges together firmly to seal them, then place this in a greaseproof (waxed) paper bag.

Cooked meats and sausages should be used within five days of purchase; cured sausages can be stored for longer, depending on whether they are whole or sliced and on the type. As a guide, sliced products should be used within a week.

Store all cooked and cured meats in the refrigerator, away from uncooked foods that may contaminate them by dripping or by direct contact.

TYPES OF CURED SAUSAGE

Some cured sausages are served finely sliced, raw, in the same way as Italian salami, others are cooked before serving. Some can be served either raw or cooked according to taste and are examples of sausages that are preserved or part-preserved. In culinary terms, the curing and aging produces a mature flavour,

which is the main characteristic now that modern refrigeration and freezing are the more practical methods for long-term preservation of meat.

Birnenformige This is a pear-shaped German salami.

Chorizo Dry sausage made of air-cured pork (or pork and beef) and pimientos. From Andalucia, this cured sausage can be eaten raw or cooked. (Longaniza is a Portugese version of chorizo.)

Coppa di Palma Also known as coppa crudo, this is cured pork collar, which is wrapped and sliced like salami.

Above: Coppa di Palma

Danish salami Danish salamis are made from pork and veal. The popular varieties are fine and fairly soft in texture, and light rather than well matured, but are usually well seasoned with spices.

Above:
Products like this sliced herb salami should be wrapped well and stored in the refrigerator. Eat within four days.

Above: Spanish lomo is made from meaty, cured pork loin.

Above: Pepperoni is a spicy Italian sausage that is often used as a topping for pizza.

Above: Salchichón is a Spanish salami.

Below: This popular French salami is made from a finely ground mixture of pork and beef and is coated with very coarsely crushed black pepper.

Felinetti
From Parma, these are delicate small salami flavoured with white wine, peppercorns and garlic.

Fiorentino This is one of the many types of flavourful salami from Tuscany in Italy. It is made with pork and other lean meats combined with fat.

French herb salami Cured meat highly flavoured with garlic, which is dried and smoked, then finished with a thick coating of herbs.

French pepper salami This popular salami is made from pork and beef, mixed with coarse chunks of fat and seasoned with whole black peppercorns.

Fuet Spanish cured sausage, long and thin in shape, and firm in texture.

Italian salami There are dozens of different regional specialities in Italy, as almost every village and town has its favourite preparation.

Kabanos There are various types of this Polish sausage, some that are suitable for cooking and others for serving cold. They are highly spiced and smoked.

Katenrauchwurst A firm, dark German sausage, made with coarsely cut, smoked pork.

Knoblauchwurst This German garlic sausage can be either poached or grilled (broiled).

Kuelbasa Made with ground pork and beef, this Polish sausage is well flavoured with garlic and seasoning.

Lomo Cured Spanish sausage made from pork loin.

Milanese salami Made with lean pork and beef, and pork fat, this is a mild Italian salami, flavoured with white wine, pepper and garlic.

Napoli Very hot Italian salami made with pork and beef seasoned with black and red pepper.

Pepperoni Made from coarsely chopped pork and beef, this Italian cured sausage is highly seasoned with ground red pepper and other spices.

Salchichón A cured sausage or salami from Spain.

Toscana A fairly coarse Italian salami seasoned with peppercorns.

TYPES OF COOKED SAUSAGE

These are ready to eat cold, sliced or spread, or they may be reheated or cooked before serving. In some cases, the first cooking is considered to be a process of blanching or light poaching and the sausage would never be served

Above: Bierschinken

without further cooking: black pudding (blood sausage) for example. Ham sausage, liver sausage and garlic sausage, plus international versions of these, are examples of popular types of cooked sausages that are ready to serve.

Bierschinken A pork and ham sausage with pistachio nuts.

Bierwurst Pork and beef sausage, which is usually quite spicy and well flavoured with garlic.

Black pudding This is a British blood sausage that is usually highly spiced

Above: Several countries make black and white puddings; these are butifarra negra and bianca from Spain.

Boudin noir This French blood sausage is poached ready for further cooking.

Butifarra bianca Spanish poached sausage. Although grouped with butifarra negra, this white sausage from Catalan is made from pork.

and dotted with fat. There are many variations. This is not strictly a fresh sausage, as it is bought poached, but it is sliced and cooked before serving.

Bockwurst A delicate white sausage made with pork and veal, chives, parsley, milk and eggs.

Boudin blanc French white pudding, made from chicken, veal, rabbit and/or pork, enriched with cream and white wine according to the particular recipe.

Above: Kalbfleischwurst

Above: Mortadella is studded with chunks of fat and pistachio nuts.

Above: Zungenwurst

Butifarra negra Spanish blood sausage, which is similar to morcilla.

Crépinette This French offal mixture is shaped into small sausages or balls and wrapped in caul fat. They are similar to British faggots. Sold ready for reheating or further cooking.

Extrawurst Large, pale pink, smooth pork and beef sausage which slices easily.

Faggots A British speciality, made from offal and highly seasoned. Traditionally wrapped in caul fat and sold cooked, ready for frying or poaching.

Frankfurter Originally this was a cold smoked sausage made with pork and salted bacon fat, but the name has since been adopted, particularly in North America, for any cooked sausage with a smoky flavour that is suitable for making hot dogs.

Haggis A Scottish sausage of lamb and lamb's offal, highly spiced and bound together with oatmeal or other cereal, is traditionally packed into a cleaned and blanched sheep's stomach ready for lengthy boiling. Nowadays, haggis is generally sold cooked, ready for further cooking or reheating.

Kalbfleischwurst Pale pink, very fine, large veal sausage.

Knoblauchwurst A sausage made from pork, peppers and spices, strongly flavoured with garlic.

Mettwurst Pork and beef sausage, which can be firm enough to slice or soft enough to spread and may be either coarse or smooth.

Morcilla A blood sausage, which is usually highly seasoned and spicy.

Mortadella A large, smooth, cooked sausage made with pork and flavoured with garlic. Studded with pistachio nuts and pieces of fat.

Pfeffer plockwurst A square sausage coated with black pepper.

Presskopf Sausage made with pork, veal and beef.

Schinken jagdwurst Made from minced (ground) pork with pork fat and ham.

Schinken kalbfleischwurst Made from minced pork, beef and veal, with pieces of ham and a little garlic.

Zungenwurst Tongue sausage, often spicy and coarse-textured.

Chinese sausages and cured meats

Wind-dried Chinese sausages are shrunken, hard and wrinkled. They are made with pork and/or offal (innards), flavoured with spices and are slightly sweet. Most large Chinese supermarkets offer a selection, some strung and hanging loose, others in shrink-wrapped packs. The sausages vary in colour from pink-red to dark brown-red and the latter tend to be made with a high percentage of offal. Check the ingredients list or go by colour, selecting the paler sausages for a light, meaty flavour or the dark colour for a distinct offal taste. The sausages are steamed for 30–45 minutes, until they are plump and tender, then sliced at a slant and served as part of a selection of cooked wind-dried foods or used in a variety of dishes. They may be stir-fried or added to braised dishes.

As well as sausages, meats and poultry are cured and dried, including pork and the rather spectacular-looking ducks, that are opened out and flattened.

TYPES OF CURED MEAT

Pork is a main ingredient for cured meat products, and is also used to make raw and cooked hams (see section on basic types of ham in previous chapter). However, there are other cured meats made using pork and meats, such as beef, venison, buffalo and poultry. The following is a small selection of the international types that are available.

Biltong Traditional African air-dried and smoked strips of beef, buffalo, antelope, venison or ostrich.

Bresaola Italian beef tenderloin, aged for a couple of months until it is a deep, rich, red colour. Good served sliced, with extra virgin olive oil, lemon juice and chopped parsley.

Bündnerfleisch Also called Bindenfleisch, this is the Swiss equivalent to bresaola. It is traditionally made only in the winter and is flavoured with white wine and treated with salt, herbs and onion before being air-dried.

Corned beef Originally derived from the word corns, the grains of salt that are used in brine prepared for salting beef, this is the north American term for salt beef or pickled beef. In Britain, the term is used exclusively for canned salt beef, which is compressed pieces of cured, cooked meat. Corned beef is generally thinly sliced and served in sandwiches or salads, but it can also be

Above: British corned beef

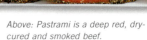

Above: Pastrami is a deep red, dry-cured and smoked beef.

chopped and pan-fried with chunks of cooked potato to make corned beef hash.

Ox tongue Sold cooked and pressed as a cold meat. This is available smoked, corned or pickled.

Pastrami This is a spiced, smoked beef, which is eaten either hot or cold. Although the name originates from the Romanian *pastrama* (from the verb *pastra*, which means to preserve), the word is Yiddish. It is famously eaten as pastrami on rye – that is, as a sandwich made with rye bread, particularly in the many Jewish delicatessens and sandwich bars of New York.

Salt beef Beef, usually brisket or silverside (pot roast), which is soaked in brine with seasonings and spices. This is available uncooked for boiling and serving hot, or sold cooked with other cold meats on deli counters. Salt beef sandwiches made with rye bread or bagels and dill pickles are a staple part of Jewish-American delicatessen cuisine.

Smoked pork loin This is a small, round nugget of lean pork, like a neat sausage.

Below: Bresaola is served sliced, with olive oil and lemon juice.

Above: Salt beef

Above: Biltong

MAKING SAUSAGES

The advantage of making sausages is that you can select high-quality meat, control the quantity of fat added and include the most wonderful mix of flavouring ingredients and seasonings (see below). Special sausage-filling equipment and machines are available, but there is no need for special utensils. Casings can be natural or synthetic and they are available from good butchers. Natural casings come salted and have to be soaked to remove excess salt and become soft.

The important point to remember when making sausages is not to overfill the casings. If there is too much mixture in the casing, the sausage cannot be twisted and separated to make individual sausages. Remember that overfilled casings will burst as the content expands during cooking.

Remember to allow enough empty casing for tying into a knot (or securing with string) before squeezing in the filling, and leave a similar length of empty casing at the end.

To make a good sausage, use good-quality ingredients. Minced (ground) pork is the traditional meat, but you can use beef, lamb or venison, as well as chicken, turkey and duck. Flavour the sausages with fresh or dried herbs and spices.

1 Soak the sausage casings in cold water for 1–2 hours. Drain and rinse the casings several times, then place in cold water until required.

2 Fit a piping (pastry) bag with a large, plain nozzle and fill with the mixture. Thread the casing on to the nozzle, pushing it as far up as possible.

3 When you cannot push any more of the casing up on to the nozzle, cut and twist or knot the end. Holding the casing on to the nozzle, squeeze the filling from the bag, allowing the casing to slide off the nozzle as it is filled.

4 When the sausage casing is full, tie the end securely to prevent the filling from escaping, then knot the other end of the casing and twist the sausage into even-size links.

COOKING SAUSAGES

The golden rule when cooking sausages is to cook them gently and thoroughly, allowing plenty of time for them to cook right through and become crisp and golden outside. Cook sausages too fiercely and the skins will split or burst, or they will overcook outside before the middle is done.

Sausages that are made with natural casings do not need to be pricked before cooking as the casings allow fat and juices to escape. Sausages made with synthetic casings should be lightly pricked before cooking, otherwise they may burst. Most sausages can be grilled (broiled), cooked on a barbecue or fried, while others, such as Bockwurst are poached. Sausages can also be added to stews or casseroles, or braised.

Grilling

Place the sausages on a rack in a grill (broiler) pan and cook well away from the heat source under a preheated grill. Cook thick sausages for about 10 minutes, turning frequently.

Frying

Pour a little oil into a frying pan, then add the sausages and cook over a low to moderate heat. Allow plenty of time for the sausages to cook through and brown evenly, turning them occasionally.

Poaching

French andouille and German sausages such as Bockwurst and frankfurters are cooked by poaching in water.

Add the sausages to a pan of hot water. Cover and simmer for about 5 minutes, depending on the size and type.

OFFAL

This is the term for the scraps, or innards, from the carcass of all kinds of meat, including sheep, pig, duck and turkey. The term covers all the edible internal organs, tail, feet and head parts. In everyday use, the term usually refers to the internal organs, such as liver, kidneys, tripe, heart and sweetbreads. Unlike meat, which has to be hung and matured before use, offal does not keep well and it has to be cooked or processed quickly. Before modern refrigeration and freezing, when an animal was slaughtered the entire carcass had to be processed promptly. The offal had to be removed, cleaned and cooked or preserved in some way. Intestines – specifically chitterlings (the small intestine) – from a pig were used not only as a casing for sausages, but also as part of the filling. Salting or curing and drying were methods used to preserve the chitterlings on their own, as well as filled sausages and meat.

Pâtés and terrines were also a means of short-term preservation: a highly seasoned liver mixture was cooked in a closed dish and air was excluded by covering the surface of the mixture with a layer of fat. Fat was an important seal for preserving cooked meat products, helping to prevent contamination.

Below: Fine-textured calf's liver (top) and lamb's liver (below).

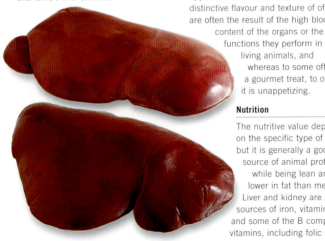

Humble or prized offerings

In Western supermarkets, where food has been sanitized and segregated from any grubby or unpleasant origins, internal organs that look unattractive are rarely displayed. Many people dislike the idea of eating organs such as head, ears, eyes or testicles, and prefer to avoid any other than neatly sliced or diced liver. In other parts of the world, not only is offal an essential food in less affluent societies, but the smaller parts can also be prized – eyes and testicles are the classic examples that are anathema to some, but considered delicacies by others. The eyes from a sheep's head are savoured in the Middle East, and by tradition are offered to the guest of honour at a meal.

In fact, the majority of offal is rich and highly flavoured, and valued in dishes, such as steak and kidney pie or pâté. Liver and kidney are the most widely used; sweetbreads, brains and heart are prepared by many traditional methods; and tripe is cooked in simple or spiced dishes loved by those who appreciate its texture and flavour. The distinctive flavour and texture of offal are often the result of the high blood content of the organs or the functions they perform in the living animals, and whereas to some offal is a gourmet treat, to others it is unappetizing.

Nutrition

The nutritive value depends on the specific type of offal, but it is generally a good source of animal protein, while being lean and lower in fat than meat. Liver and kidney are rich sources of iron, vitamin A and some of the B complex vitamins, including folic acid.

Above: The unusual honeycomb texture of tripe means that, like other types of offal, it is an acquired taste.

Buying

Offal should always be fresh. Check sell-by dates on pre-packed offal and buy from a supermarket where the offal is neatly displayed in uncluttered refrigerators that are not overfilled. When buying offal loose from a butcher, it should always look fresh, moist and clean, with an even colour and texture. Whole organs or cuts should not be damaged and they should not be sitting in puddles of blood. Offal should always smell fresh – never buy offal that has a pronounced, stale odour. Buy only from a butcher who clearly stores, prepares and displays offal in hygienic, cold conditions. The seller should have a speedy turnover.

Foie gras

In France, where *foie gras* is a speciality, varieties of goose are bred especially for this purpose. Fattened goose liver is pale and creamy in texture. It tastes wonderful and is considered a great delicacy by many gourmets. However, the way it is produced makes it a controversial ingredient in some parts of the world.

Storing

Always leave sealed, pre-packed offal in its container and use it by the date given on the packet. Transfer offal bought loose to a deep dish and cover it tightly with clear film (plastic wrap) or a close-fitting lid. Use loose offal within 24 hours of purchase. Store the offal in the refrigerator, in the coldest part and where any drips which may escape will not be bale to contaminate other foods.

THE DIFFERENT TYPES OF OFFAL

Liver

The fine, close texture and pronounced, fairly "dry" flavour of liver makes it probably the most popular and versatile of offal. Calf's liver has the finest texture and lightest flavour. It is comparatively expensive and regarded as a prime cut in Western cooking. Lamb's liver also has a fairly mild flavour. It is cheap, readily available and widely used as a main ingredient in its own right, as well as for pâtés. Pig's and ox liver are strong in flavour and they have a coarser texture. Pig's liver is a particularly good ingredient for rich pâtés. Chicken, turkey and duck livers are similar in size, flavour and texture. They are significantly lighter in flavour, fine-textured and rich, and are more versatile than the other types of liver. Goose liver is larger and paler in colour (see box on *foie gras*, left).

Above: Ox (top) and veal kidneys

Above, clockwise from top left: chicken, goose (foie gras), turkey and duck livers

Right: Lamb's kidneys (bottom) have a more delicate flavour than pig's kidneys.

Above: Ox liver

Below: The strong flavour of pig's liver means that it is excellent for making pâté.

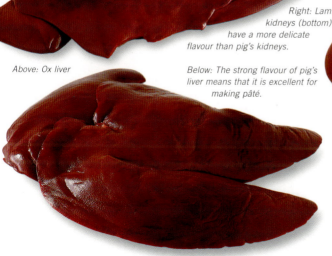

Kidney

Kidney has a distinctive taste that varies according to type. Lamb's kidneys are small, tender and comparatively delicate in flavour. They are often cooked halved or whole. Veal kidneys are very tender. Ox kidney is strongly flavoured and firm. It is the classic ingredient for steak and kidney pie (although lamb's kidneys are often used for a lighter flavour). Pig's kidney, which has a strong, robust flavour, is used in terrines and French *charcuterie*.

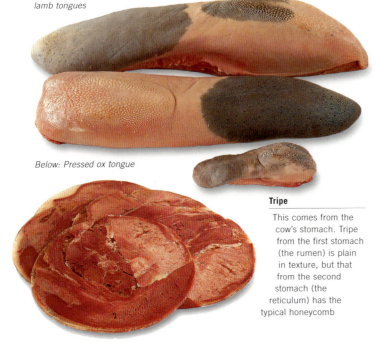

Tail

Oxtail has a fairly large amount of creamy-white fat covering a modest amount of dark red meat, with about an equal proportion of meat to bone. It requires long, moist cooking. Oxtail has a rich flavour.

Above: Oxtail is generally sold cut into thick pieces ready for braising or stewing.

Below: Shin bones from cattle are the source of bone marrow, which is used to enrich soups and stews.

Tongue

Ox (beef) tongue is sold fresh or cured in brine; veal tongue is popular in France. A large tongue is part-boiled so that the thick layer of skin can be removed, then the remaining, trimmed, meat requires lengthy cooking until tender. It can be used in hot dishes or pressed and served as a cold meat (a particular British speciality). Small lamb's tongues can be casseroled.

Below, from top: Ox, veal and lamb tongues

Below: Pressed ox tongue

Bone marrow

Found in hollow bones, particularly shin bones, from cow or calf carcasses, this pale, fatty substance has a full flavour. When poached, marrow can be scooped out and used to enrich soups, stews, sauces and risottos. It is also served hot as a spread or as a topping for canapés. Bone marrow is a prized part of the Italian veal casserole *osso bucco*, in which slices of veal are cooked on the bone.

Tripe

This comes from the cow's stomach. Tripe from the first stomach (the rumen) is plain in texture, but that from the second stomach (the reticulum) has the typical honeycomb texture. It is sold cleaned, washed and blanched (or often fully cooked), when it is creamy white in colour. It is easily digestible and very nutritious. Tripe has a distinctive flavour – not strong in the same way as liver or kidney, but pronounced and determined to dominate even spicy sauces. It is usually stewed, either with onions in milk to make a pale *blanquette* or in a spicy tomato sauce with onions and dried mushrooms in Polish style.

Head

Brains and tongue are treated as separate types of offal from the head. Sheep's head is a traditional ingredient for making broth or soup all over Europe. Calf's and pig's heads are traditionally used for making brawn. The heads are boiled until the meat is falling off the bone. The stock is then strained, the meat picked over, chopped, then set in the broth.

A pig's head can be ordered and the butcher will chop it into chunks that are not too ghastly for the squeamish to handle. The meat from pig's head makes delicious brawn or if potted to a firmer pâté, a dish known as pork cheese. The cheek when cured as a ham is known as a bath chap: a small ham covered with fat and coated with breadcrumbs; these are available from some traditional butchers.

*Left: Cow's feet
(top) and pig's
trotters (feet)*

Sweetbreads

The thymus glands taken from the neck
and heart of young animals, such as
calves and lambs. Pink and delicate
with a tender, meaty texture when
cooked by braising or boiling, they are
often pressed and fried after blanching.

Brains

Lamb and veal brains are pale pink and
delicate. Once rinsed, soaked and
blanched they can be fried or braised.

Trotters and feet

Pig's trotters (feet) and calf's feet
can be bought whole or split
in half. They are boiled
to make stocks that
set firmly when
cold. They can
also be used to
enrich stews or
soups; cooked and
jellied, then served
cold; or grilled.

*Above: Calf's
and lamb's
sweetbreads*

*Right: Lights are popular in many
countries, but in Britain and America
they are used to make pet food.*

Lights

These are the lungs of an animal. In
Britain and America they are usually
sold for pet food, but they are used in
traditional dishes in some countries.
Lamb or pork lights may be served with
a piquant sauce, added to stews or
used for making pork *pâté de foie*.

Heart

This is nutritious and with very little
waste. Lamb heart is the most tender
and lightest in flavour. Pork or pig's
heart is larger and slightly coarser;
beef or ox heart is big but not
very tender, while chicken heart
is very small and usually sold as
part of the giblets with a cleaned
bird. All need long, slow cooking and
careful trimming.

Above: Tiny chicken hearts

Chitterlings

These are pig's intestines used
as sausage casings or chopped
up as part of the filling. They
can also be blanched and
grilled (broiled) or fried. They are
particularly popular in France,
Greece and North America.

*Right, clockwise from top: Ox, pig
and lamb hearts are extremely
nutritious, but need long, slow cooking.*

PREPARING AND COOKING OFFAL

Offal (innards) is generally easy to prepare and cook. The majority of types are sold trimmed and ready to prepare and cook, and some, such as tripe, are sold blanched or completely cooked.

Offal can be cooked in a variety of ways: poaching suits many cuts, especially tongue and brains, robust cuts, such as heart, can be braised, while liver, kidneys and sweetbreads are good pan-fried in butter.

Trimming liver

The majority of liver is sold trimmed and ready to cook, but it is still a good idea to check for any stray tubes or areas of skin before cooking.

1 Trim off any patches of pale gristle or small pieces of tube that may still be attached. Use a small, pointed knife to cut out the trimmings.

2 A fine skin or membrane sometimes remains on the surface of the liver, often in patches where it has not been thoroughly trimmed. Rub your fingertips over the liver to feel the skin, then gently pull any excess away. For pan-frying, cut the liver into neat, even slices, about 1cm/½in thick. Cut slightly thicker slices for grilling (broiling).

Frying liver

Liver should be cooked through but it should be still slightly pink – not rare – in the middle, when it will still be tender. If the liver is cooked over a medium heat for too long, it will become tough and dry out before it browns.

Melt a little butter in a heavy frying pan and add the liver when it is foaming and hot. Cook briefly over a fairly high heat until it is browned underneath, then, using tongs, turn the liver over and cook the slices on the second side. If you prefer to grill (broil) liver, brush it with a little melted butter or vegetable oil and cook under a hot grill (broiler) for 3–4 minutes on each side.

Trimming kidneys

Kidneys are surrounded by a pad of firm, creamy fat, which is usually removed before they are sold. The fat from ox (beef) kidneys is used for suet.

1 If the fat is still in place, snip or cut it, then slide and pull it away from around the kidney. Carefully peel off the thin membrane covering the kidney. A white core of membrane and tubes lies in the middle of the kidney – it looks like a solid fatty lump – and this should be removed before cooking.

2 Cut the kidney in half using a sharp knife – here a lamb's kidney is being split lengthways.

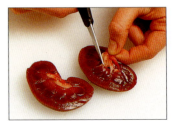

3 Use sharp kitchen scissors to snip out the tubes and pale core. If they are not removed, these are unpleasant and tough in the cooked kidney.

Cooking kidneys

Lamb's kidneys are tender and they cook quickly. Griddling is a good alternative to pan-frying or grilling. Heat the griddle until very hot, then add a little butter or oil and heat it again for a few seconds.

Lay the halved kidneys on the griddle, cut sides down, and cook until browned and firm underneath. Turn and cook the second side until browned. The kidneys feel just firm when cooked.

Cooking tongue

Ox (beef) tongue is sold cleaned and ready to cook, usually with the root trimmed off the end.

1 Place the tongue in a large pan with cold water to cover. Add flavouring ingredients such as carrot, celery, onion and a bouquet garni of powerful, aromatic herbs, such as sage, thyme, bay leaves and rosemary.

2 Bring slowly to the boil, skim off any surface scum, then reduce the heat so that the water simmers steadily. At this stage, spices, such as peppercorns, cloves, coriander seeds and juniper berries can be added. Cover and simmer for 3–4 hours, or until the meat is tender. Leave the tongue to cool in its cooking liquid until it is just cool enough to handle.

3 Drain the tongue and discard the cooking liquid. Cut away any tough, white gristle at the wide end of the tongue, if necessary (this root may already have been removed). Then peel off the thick skin. The tongue is then ready for cutting up and reheating in a sauce or it can be curled into a small round dish or tin and weighted, then allowed to cool completely.

4 Pressed tongue should be unmoulded and sliced thinly, then it can be served in the same way as cooked ham. It is excellent with mustard or pickles.

Pot-roasting pig's trotters

Trotters (feet) are sold cleaned and ready for cooking. Rinse and dry them, then singe off any hairs by going over the surface of the skin with a lighted taper or match. Heat a little oil in a large, flameproof casserole and brown the trotters on all sides. Remove them from the casserole and set aside. Add thickly sliced onions, carrots, peeled garlic cloves and herbs, such as bay leaves, sage and thyme, to the casserole, then replace the trotters on the bed of vegetables and herbs. Pour in enough water, stock or wine (or a mixture) to cover the vegetables. Cover and cook in the oven at 180°C/350°F/Gas 4 for about 2 hours, turning the trotters occasionally, until they are golden brown and tender.

Extracting marrow from bones

Ask the butcher to saw the marrow-bones into pieces about 7.5cm/3in long. To serve the bone marrow as a starter or a spread for toast, brush the bones with oil and roast at 200°C/400°F/Gas 6 for 45 minutes, or until well browned. The bones may also be roasted at the same time as a joint of meat.

Alternatively, poach the bones in a large pan of salted boiling water for about 3 minutes to soften the marrow, then drain well and use a teaspoon to scoop out the marrow. Poached bone marrow can be used to enrich stock, sauce or risotto, or it can be seasoned and served as a spread.

Preparing sweetbreads

1 Soak the sweetbreads in cold water for 2 hours, changing the water several times. Rinse the sweetbreads well: they are ready for cooking when all signs of blood have been soaked or rinsed away. Drain, then place in a pan and pour in cold water to cover. Bring to the boil, then immediately reduce the heat and simmer for 5 minutes, or until the sweetbreads are firm and white.

2 Drain the sweetbreads and peel off the membrane, then remove any pieces of gristle or fat and ducts. Cool and chill until firm. When firm, the sweetbreads can be sliced or cut into pieces, coated in a little flour and pan-fried or sautéed in butter, then simmered in a sauce. Sweetbreads are also good coated in egg and breadcrumbs, shallow fried and served with lemon wedges.

Preparing brains

These are prepared in the same way as sweetbreads, by thorough rinsing, soaking and blanching, then trimming. They are then either poached in a sauce until tender or lightly pressed under weights until cold, when they can be sliced and coated with breadcrumbs and pan-fried. Brains have a creamy texture when cooked.

STOCKS, SAUCES AND GRAVIES

A well-flavoured stock is one of the basic foundations of good cooking, and is used in a whole

range of meat dishes, from soups and stews to pot-roasts. Sauces and gravies are an equally

important part of meat cooking, and stock forms the base

for many of these recipes, too.

STOCKS

We use the word stock simply because it was something most cooks kept a stock of for use in the kitchen. These days, sadly, it tends to mean something you get when you add a kettleful of boiling water to a stock cube (or a bouillon cube as it is called in the United States and France).

Traditionally, stock was the product of a pot kept simmering on the hob (stovetop) to which leftover pieces of meat, as well as bones, vegetables, vegetable trimmings and herbs, were added. The cook then always had a stock of broth, packed with flavour, to use as a basis for soups, stews and sauces. These days few households have a stockpot on the go and small batches are usually made as and when required. Nevertheless, a good, home-made stock has much more flavour than a cube and it is well worth the effort of making your own.

A well-flavoured stock is the basis of good cooking – which is why young chefs are always judged by the quality of the stocks they make – and if a stock is poor, then the resulting soups, casseroles, sauces and gravies coming out of the restaurant kitchen will be poor, too. That's why, although stocks are not difficult to make, professional chefs spend so long getting them right.

There are, basically, two different types of stock: a brown stock in which the bones are browned in the oven first, and a white stock in which the bones are poached rather than roasted. Brown stocks are normally made from beef and lamb and are used for making consommés, soups, and dark sauces and for cooking with dark meats. White stocks are made from veal bones and are used for making soups, white sauces and for cooking with young, tender meats.

The reason people go wrong when making stock is that they think it's just a pot for leftovers. It was, historically, but the way to get a really good stock is to use fresh bones and vegetables. Never add salt to a stock until the end of cooking and always use whole peppercorns because ground pepper will only make the stock taste bitter.

Basic meat stock

MAKES ABOUT 1 LITRE/1¾ PINTS/4 CUPS

INGREDIENTS
675g/1½lb beef or veal bones
1 large onion, quartered
1 celery stick, sliced
1 carrot, thickly sliced
6 peppercorns
bouquet garni or a selection of fresh herbs, such as parsley, thyme and rosemary

1 Use a meat cleaver to chop up larger bones so that they will fit easily into your largest pan (or get your butcher to do this). (Cutting the bones into pieces helps to extract the collagen and impart the maximum possible flavour during cooking.)

2 Transfer the bones and vegetables to the pan. Add the peppercorns, bouquet garni or herbs and 1.5–1.75 litres/2½–3 pints/6¼–7½ cups water to cover. Bring to the boil and, using a slotted spoon, skim off as much of the scum as possible.

3 Partially cover the pan and simmer gently (don't let it come to the boil again or the stock will become cloudy) for 2–3 hours.

4 Strain the liquid through a fine strainer into a large, heatproof bowl, then gently press the bones and vegetables to extract as much flavour as possible (but not so hard that the vegetables start to go into the stock).

5 Leave the liquid to cool, then chill overnight (the fat will rise to the top and can easily be removed). If you don't have time to let the stock cool, skim off as much fat as possible with a spoon and then draw absorbent kitchen paper carefully across the top of the stock to draw up any remaining surface fat.

6 Store in the refrigerator and boil up every day, or freeze. When needed, heat the stock and taste to check its flavour. If it tastes very weak, simmer to reduce; this concentrates its flavour. Season to taste with salt and pepper.

Bouquet garni

This is a French term for a bundle of fresh or dried herbs – often parsley, thyme, chervil and chives and sometimes whole cloves and unskinned garlic. This is added to the stockpot to impart extra flavour to the stock.

Basic veal stock

MAKES ABOUT 1 LITRE/1¾ PINTS/4 CUPS

INGREDIENTS
    6 kg/2¼lb veal bones
    1 large onion, quartered
    1 celery stick, sliced
    1 carrot, thickly sliced
    6 peppercorns
    1 garlic clove
    bouquet garni

1 Using a cleaver, chop the veal bones into rough pieces and put in a large pan. (If you don't have a strong enough knife, or are unsure of doing this yourself, or when purchasing the veal, ask your butcher to chop the bones into pieces that are small enough to fit into your stock pot). Cover the bones with plenty of water.

2 Add the vegetables, peppercorns, garlic and bouquet garni to the pan and bring slowly to the boil.

3 Using a slotted spoon, skim well, removing as much scum as possible, and simmer gently for at least 2–3 hours. Simmer slowly, if possible, as this will help to reduce the stock without clouding.

4 Strain, and taste for flavour. If not strong enough, boil for a little longer. Gently press the bones and vegetables to extract as much flavour as possible (but don't push so hard that the vegetables start to go into the stock).

5 Leave the liquid to cool completely, then chill it overnight (the fat will rise to the top, then solidify, when it can easily be removed).

6 If you don't have time to let the stock cool, skim off as much fat as possible with a spoon and then carefully draw absorbent kitchen paper across the top of the stock to remove the surface fat. Store in the refrigerator and boil up every day, or freeze.

COOK'S TIPS
Another way of removing fat from stock is to drop a couple of ice cubes into cold stock. The fat will cling to the ice cubes and set, and both ice cubes and fat can then be discarded.
For a brown veal stock, roast the bones first in the oven at 230°C/450°F/Gas 8 for 30–40 minutes, until well browned. Add the vegetables and brown them also, for a further 15–20 minutes. Browning will give the stock additional flavour and colour. Transfer all the ingredients to a pot. Discard any fat from the pan. Add the water and flavourings as before and make up a stock.

Brown meat stock

MAKES ABOUT 1 LITRE/1¾ PINTS/4 CUPS

INGREDIENTS
    675g/1½lb beef or veal bones
    1 large onion, quartered
    1 celery stick, sliced
    1 carrot, thickly sliced
    6 peppercorns
    bouquet garni

1 Use a cleaver to chop up the larger beef or veal bones so they will fit easily into your largest pan. (Cutting the bones into small pieces helps to extract the collagen and impart the maximum possible flavour during cooking.) Put the bones and vegetables in a large, roasting pan.

2 Cook the bones and vegetables in a preheated oven at 230°C/450°F/Gas 8, stirring frequently, until browned.

3 Transfer the bones and vegetables to a large pan. Add the peppercorns, bouquet garni and 1.5–1.75 litres/ 2½–3 pints/6¼–7½ cups water to cover. Bring to the boil, skim well to remove as much scum as possible and simmer gently (don't let it boil again or the stock will become cloudy) for 2–3 hours.

4 Strain the liquid, then gently press the bones and vegetables to extract as much flavour as possible (but don't push so hard that the vegetables start to go into the stock). Discard the bones and vegetables.

5 Leave the liquid to cool, then chill overnight (the fat will rise to the top and can then easily be removed). If you don't have time to let it cool, skim off as much fat as possible with a spoon and then draw kitchen paper carefully across the top of the stock to remove the surface fat. Store in the refrigerator and boil up every day, or freeze.

> **Other stock bones**
> Beef and veal bones are the best choice for stock. It is not usual to make stock using ham bones because they are so salty. Lamb bones are not used because of their strong flavour, but can be mixed with other bones. Pork bones are usually mixed with other meat bones because they make the stock very sweet.

SAUCES

The classic sauces of France were invented to enhance the flavour of meat and are indispensable in meat cooking.

White sauce

The basic roux-based milk sauce.

MAKES ABOUT 600ML/1 PINT/2½ CUPS

INGREDIENTS
  50g/2oz/¼ cup butter
  30ml/2 tbsp plain (all-purpose) flour
  600ml/1 pint/2½ cups milk
  salt and ground white pepper

1 Melt the butter in a small pan.

2 Add the flour and cook for 1 minute, stirring constantly.

3 Turn off the heat and gradually stir in the milk.

4 Return the pan to the heat, bring the sauce to the boil, stirring constantly.

5 Simmer gently for 1 minute and season. This makes a coating sauce. To make a thin, pouring sauce, add another 300ml/½ pint/1¼ cups milk.

Béchamel sauce

Follow the recipe for white sauce, but add 1 quartered onion, 1 sliced carrot, 1 sliced celery stick, 1 bay leaf and 6 peppercorns to the milk. Boil, infuse for 30 minutes, then strain.

Parsley sauce

This is the traditional sauce to serve with ham and bacon dishes.

Follow the recipe for white sauce and add 30ml/2 tbsp finely chopped parsley with the salt and pepper.

Mushroom sauce

This is a perfect accompaniment for griddled or pan-fried steaks.

Follow the recipe for white sauce but first pan-fry 115g/4oz/1⅔ cups sliced mushrooms, such as shiitake, and 1 chopped garlic clove. Stir the mushroom mixture into the white sauce.

Onion sauce

This is good served with liver and grilled (broiled) meats. Follow the recipe for white sauce, but first cook 1 finely chopped onion in the butter.

Horseradish cream sauce

The traditional sauce for roast beef.

MAKES ABOUT 300ML/½ PINT/1¼ CUPS

INGREDIENTS
  300ml/½ pint/1¼ cups double
    (heavy) cream
  25g/1oz fresh horseradish, grated
  pinch each sugar and
    mustard powder
  dash of vinegar

Whip the cream to soft peaks, then fold into the grated horseradish. Add the sugar, mustard powder and vinegar to taste.

Béarnaise sauce

This classic, hot, creamy sauce, which takes its name from Béarn in south-west France, is ideal to serve with griddled, grilled (broiled), pan-fried or roast beef. Add the butter, dice by dice, or the mixture will curdle.

MAKES ABOUT 450ML/¾ PINT/2 CUPS

INGREDIENTS
  90ml/6 tbsp white wine vinegar
  12 black peppercorns
  2 bay leaves
  2 shallots, finely chopped
  4 fresh tarragon sprigs
  4 egg yolks
  225g/8oz/1 cup unsalted (sweet)
    butter, softened and diced
  30ml/2 tbsp chopped fresh tarragon
  salt and ground white pepper

1 Put the vinegar, peppercorns, bay leaves, shallots and tarragon in a small pan and simmer until reduced to 30ml/2 tbsp. Strain through a sieve.

2 Beat the egg yolks in a heatproof bowl, set over a pan of very gently simmering water. Season. Beat in the strained vinegar mixture, then the butter, dice by dice. Add the tarragon, then serve at once.

Mint sauce

The classic accompaniment to roast lamb.

MAKES ABOUT 90ML/6 TBSP

INGREDIENTS
  bunch of mint, about 15g/½oz
  10ml/2 tsp caster (superfine) sugar
  15ml/1 tbsp boiling water
  30ml/2 tbsp white wine vinegar

Finely chop the mint with the sugar. Add the boiling water and mix, stirring until the sugar has dissolved. Add the vinegar 15ml/1 tbsp at a time. Leave the sauce to stand until ready to serve.

Apple sauce

This is the perfect accompaniment to serve with roast or grilled (broiled) pork.

MAKES ABOUT 300ML/½ PINT/1¼ CUPS

INGREDIENTS
  450g/1lb tart cooking apples
  30ml/2 tbsp (hard) cider
    or water
  25g/1oz/2 tbsp soft light brown
    sugar, or to taste
  25g/1oz/2 tbsp butter

1 Peel the apples, remove the cores and chop the apples into large chunks.

2 Put the apples, cider and sugar in a pan. Cook for 5–10 minutes, until soft.

3 Beat well with a wooden spoon or blend in a food processor depending on whether you like your apple sauce chunky or smooth. Beat in the butter and reheat, if necessary.

Cranberry sauce

This is the traditional accompaniment for baked ham.

MAKES ABOUT 600ML/1 PINT/2½ CUPS

INGREDIENTS
  350g/12oz/3 cups fresh or
    frozen cranberries
  175g/6oz/scant 1 cup golden
    caster (superfine) sugar
  15ml/1 tbsp Cointreau
  1.5ml/¼ tsp mixed (apple pie) spice
  grated rind of 2 oranges
  50ml/2fl oz/¼ cup orange juice
  ground black pepper

Put all the ingredients in a large heavy pan. Cook gently over a low heat until the sugar is completely dissolved, stirring frequently. Bring to the boil, then reduce the heat slightly and simmer, stirring occasionally, for 20–25 minutes, or until thickened.

Tomato sauce

This is delicious served with pork, lamb and sausages.

MAKES ABOUT 1.2 LITRES/2 PINTS/5 CUPS

INGREDIENTS
    900g/2lb ripe tomatoes, quartered
    225g/8oz onions, finely chopped
    450g/1lb cooking apples, peeled,
      cored and finely chopped
    1.2 litres/2 pints/5 cups distilled
      white vinegar
    25g/1oz mustard seeds, crushed
    1 dried chilli
    5cm/2in piece cinnamon stick
    3 blades mace
    6 peppercorns
    2.5ml/½ tsp grated nutmeg
    50g/2oz/¼ cup sea salt
    225g/8oz/generous 1 cup golden
      granulated sugar

1 Put the tomatoes in a preserving pan. Add the onions and apples and half the vinegar. Stir in the spices, flavourings and salt. Bring the mixture slowly to the boil and simmer for about 1–1½ hours, or until reduced by about one-third.

2 Sieve the pulp. Return the tomato mixture to the pan with the remaining vinegar and the sugar and stir over a low heat until the sugar has dissolved. Bring to the boil and simmer for 30 minutes, or until thickened. Pour into sterilized, warmed bottles and seal. Store for up to 1 week.

Orange sauce

A tangy sauce for ham and gammon.

MAKES ABOUT 450ML/¾ PINT/2 CUPS

INGREDIENTS
    25g/1oz/2 tbsp butter
    40g/1½oz/⅓ cup plain (all-purpose)
      white flour
    300ml/½ pint/1¼ cups veal stock
    150ml/¼ pint/⅔ cup red wine
    2 oranges
    10ml/2 tsp lemon juice
    15ml/1 tbsp orange-flavoured liqueur
    30ml/2 tbsp redcurrant jelly
    salt and ground black pepper

1 Melt the butter in a small pan over a medium heat. Add the flour and cook for about 3 minutes, stirring constantly, until lightly browned.

2 Without heating, gradually stir in the stock and red wine. Bring to the boil, stirring, then simmer for 5 minutes.

3 Thinly peel the orange rind from 1 of the oranges using a swivel-bladed peeler. Put the rind in a pan, cover with cold water and bring to the boil. Cook for 5 minutes, then drain.

4 Meanwhile, squeeze the juice from both oranges into the sauce. Add the lemon juice, orange-flavoured liqueur and orange rind, with the redcurrant jelly. Stir the sauce, then reheat gently. Season to taste with salt and pepper before serving.

Bread sauce

Traditionally served with turkey, this sauce is equally good with sausages.

MAKES ABOUT 450ML/¾ PINT/2 CUPS

INGREDIENTS
    1 onion, studded with 6 cloves
    1 bay leaf
    300ml/½ pint/1¼ cups milk
    150ml/¼ pint/⅔ cup single
      (light) cream
    115g/4oz/2 cups white breadcrumbs
    knob (pat) of butter
    salt and ground black pepper

1 Put the clove-studded onion, bay leaf and milk in a pan and bring slowly to the boil. Remove from the heat and leave to stand for at least 30 minutes to allow the flavour of the onion to infuse into the milk.

2 Strain the milk and discard the clove-studded onion and the bay leaf. Pour the milk into a clean pan and add the cream and breadcrumbs. Bring slowly to the boil, then reduce the heat and simmer gently for 5 minutes.

3 Stir in the butter and season with a little salt and pepper to taste just before serving.

GRAVIES

The classic gravies, served with meat dishes by Auguste Escoffier at the Savoy and the Ritz Carlton in the 1890s, are a world away from the gravy that comes by adding boiling water to stock (bouillon) cubes or freeze-dried gravy granules. The traditional British meat gravy – which ranges in colour from pale gold to dark brown – is made with what is left in the base of the pan after a joint has been roasted, deglazed with good stock and carefully seasoned. Some gravies are really quite thick, others rather thin; it is really a matter of personal preference. Many cooks add a spoonful of flour to help thicken the gravy although purists condemn this.

In France, *jus de viande* is a version of a thin British gravy. Red eye gravy, famous in the American south for being served with ham and other pork dishes, is made by adding a little water (or, sometimes, strong black coffee) to the roasting pan and simmering it until it bubbles and turns red. Another version adds a teaspoon of brown sugar, stirred until it caramelizes, before the water is added.

Thickened gravy

This classic gravy is perfect to serve with all roast meats.

MAKES ABOUT 450ML/¾ PINT/2 CUPS

INGREDIENTS
   60ml/4 tbsp plain (all-purpose) flour
   450ml/¾ pint/scant 2 cups good-
     quality stock
   45ml/3 tbsp port or sherry
   salt and ground black pepper

1 Tilt the roasting pan slightly and spoon off almost all the fat, leaving the meat juices behind.

2 Sprinkle the flour into the pan and heat gently for 1 minute, stirring constantly. Gradually add the stock, stirring constantly until thickened. Add the port or sherry, season with salt and pepper and simmer gently for about 1–2 minutes. Taste and adjust the seasoning, if necessary. Serve hot.

Onion gravy

This is the ideal gravy to serve with fried or grilled (broiled) sausages and liver.

MAKES ABOUT 450ML/¾ PINT/2 CUPS

INGREDIENTS
   30ml/2 tbsp olive oil
   25g/1oz/2 tbsp butter
   8 onions, sliced
   5ml/1 tsp caster (superfine) sugar
   15ml/1 tbsp plain (all-purpose) flour
   300ml/½ pint/1¼ cups brown
     meat stock
   salt and ground black pepper

1 Heat the oil and butter in a pan until foaming, then add the onions. Mix well, so the onions are coated in the butter mixture. Cover the pan and cook gently for 30 minutes, stirring frequently. Add the sugar and cook for a further 5 minutes; the onions will soften, caramelize and reduce.

2 Turn off the heat and stir in the flour.

3 Gradually add the stock and return the pan to the heat. Bring the onion gravy to the boil, stirring constantly.

4 Simmer for 2–3 minutes, or until thickened, then season with salt and pepper to taste.

> **A glaze** is used to give a dish an especially smooth, shiny (and sometimes transparent) finish. A meat glaze is made by the prolonged reduction of meat stock, resulting in a syrupy liquid. Alcohol, such as Madeira, is often added to the reduction and a little butter, whisked in at the end, to give a smooth, satiny appearance.

BEEF AND VEAL DISHES

These succulent meats have terrific taste and texture. The wide range of cuts available means

that they are also extremely versatile, suitable for every kind of meal, from quick and easy

suppers to Sunday lunch. This chapter includes the time-honoured classic Roast Rib of Beef

with Yorkshire puddings, as well as great traditional dishes, such as Boeuf Bourguignonne,

Steak Béarnaise and Osso Bucco with Risotto Milanese. But although beef and veal are great

meats for robust, classic dishes, both can also be used to make light and modern meals that are

quick and easy to cook, such as Italian Meatballs or Chunky Burgers with Spicy Relish.

ROAST RIB OF BEEF

THIS JOINT LOOKS SPECTACULAR, AND SERVED IN TRADITIONAL STYLE, WITH YORKSHIRE PUDDINGS AND HORSERADISH SAUCE, IT MAKES A PERFECT CELEBRATION MEAL.

SERVES EIGHT TO TEN

INGREDIENTS
    45ml/3 tbsp mixed peppercorns
    15ml/1 tbsp juniper berries
    2.75kg/6lb rolled rib of beef
    30ml/2 tbsp Dijon mustard
    15ml/1 tbsp olive oil
For the Yorkshire puddings
    150ml/¼ pint/⅔ cup water
    150ml/¼ pint/⅔ cup milk
    115g/4oz/1 cup plain
      (all-purpose) flour
    pinch of salt
    2 eggs, beaten
    60ml/4 tbsp lard (shortening),
      melted, or sunflower oil (optional)
For the caramelized shallots
    20 shallots
    5 garlic cloves, peeled
    60ml/4 tbsp light olive oil
    15ml/1 tbsp caster (superfine) sugar
For the gravy
    150ml/¼ pint/⅔ cup red wine
    600ml/1 pint/2½ cups beef stock
    salt and ground black pepper

1 Preheat the oven to 230°C/450°F/ Gas 8. Crush the peppercorns and juniper berries. Sprinkle half the spices over the meat. Transfer to a roasting pan and roast for 30 minutes.

COOK'S TIP
If you prefer to cook beef on the bone, buy a 3.6kg/8lb forerib. Trim off the excess fat, scatter over the spices, then follow the instructions in steps 1 and 2. Roast at the lower temperature for 2 hours for rare beef, 2½ hours for medium rare, and 3 hours for well done.

2 Reduce the oven temperature to 180°C/350°F/Gas 4. Mix the mustard and oil into the remaining crushed spices and spread the resulting paste over the meat. Roast the meat for a further 1¼ hours if you like your meat rare, 1 hour 50 minutes for a medium-rare result or 2 hours 25 minutes for a joint that is medium to well done. Baste the joint frequently during cooking.

3 Make the Yorkshire puddings as soon as the beef is in the oven. Stir the water into the milk. Sift the flour and salt into a bowl. Make a well in the middle and gradually whisk in the eggs, followed by the milk and water to make a smooth batter. Cover and leave to stand for about 1 hour. (The batter can be made well in advance and chilled overnight in the refrigerator if convenient.)

4 An hour before the beef is due to be ready, mix the shallots and garlic cloves with the light olive oil and spoon into the roasting pan around the beef. After about 30 minutes, lightly sprinkle the sugar over the shallots and garlic, and stir the shallots and garlic 2–3 times during cooking.

5 Transfer the meat to a serving platter, cover tightly with foil and set aside in a warm place for 20–30 minutes. (This resting time makes carving easier.) Increase the oven temperature to 230°C/450°F/Gas 8. Divide 60ml/4 tbsp dripping from the meat or the lard or oil, if using, among 10 individual Yorkshire pudding pans or 16 large patty tins (muffin pans), and heat in the oven for about 5 minutes.

6 Spoon the Yorkshire pudding batter into the hot fat in the tins and bake for 20–30 minutes, or until risen, firm and golden brown. The time depends on the size of the tins: larger Yorkshire puddings will take longer than those in patty tins.

7 Make the gravy while the Yorkshire puddings are cooking. Simmer the red wine and beef stock together in a pan for about 5 minutes to intensify the flavour of the gravy.

8 Skim the fat from the meat juices in the roasting pan, then pour in the wine mixture and simmer until the gravy is reduced and thickened slightly to a syrupy consistency. Stir frequently with a wooden spoon to remove all of the roasting residue from the roasting pan. Season to taste.

9 Serve the beef with the individual Yorkshire puddings, caramelized shallots and gravy. Offer roast potatoes or game chips as accompaniments along with a selection of lightly cooked, seasonal vegetables.

BOEUF BOURGUIGNONNE

THE CLASSIC FRENCH DISH OF BEEF COOKED IN BURGUNDY STYLE, WITH RED WINE, SMALL PIECES OF BACON, SHALLOTS AND MUSHROOMS, IS COOKED FOR SEVERAL HOURS AT A LOW TEMPERATURE. USING TOP RUMP OR BRAISING STEAK REDUCES THE COOKING TIME.

SERVES SIX

INGREDIENTS
  175g/6oz rindless streaky (fatty)
    bacon rashers (strips), chopped
  900g/2lb lean braising steak, such
    as top rump (rump roast) of beef or
    braising steak
  30ml/2 tbsp plain (all-purpose) flour
  45ml/3 tbsp sunflower oil
  25g/1oz/2 tbsp butter
  12 shallots
  2 garlic cloves, crushed
  175g/6oz/2⅓ cups mushrooms, sliced
  450ml/¾ pint/scant 2 cups robust
    red wine
  150ml/¼ pint/⅔ cup beef stock
    or consommé
  1 bay leaf
  2 sprigs each of fresh thyme, parsley
    and marjoram
  salt and ground black pepper

1 Preheat the oven to 160°C/325°F/ Gas 3. Heat a large flameproof casserole, then add the bacon and cook, stirring occasionally, until the pieces are crisp and golden brown.

2 Meanwhile, cut the meat into 2.5cm/ 1in cubes. Season the flour and use to coat the meat. Use a slotted spoon to remove the bacon from the casserole and set aside. Add and heat the oil, then brown the beef in batches and set aside with the bacon.

VARIATION
Use lardons, which are available from large supermarkets, instead of the bacon.

3 Add the butter to the fat remaining in the casserole. Cook the shallots and garlic until just starting to colour, then add the mushrooms and cook for a further 5 minutes. Replace the bacon and meat, and stir in the wine and stock or consommé. Tie the bay leaf, thyme, parsley and marjoram together into a bouquet garni and add to the casserole.

4 Cover and cook in the oven for 1½ hours, or until the meat is tender, stirring once or twice. Season to taste and serve the casserole with creamy mashed root vegetables, such as celeriac and potatoes.

COOK'S TIP
Boeuf Bourguignonne freezes very well. Transfer the mixture to a dish so that it cools quickly, then pour it into a rigid plastic container. Push all the cubes of meat down into the sauce or they will dry out. Freeze for up to 2 months. Thaw overnight in the refrigerator, then transfer to a flameproof casserole and add 150ml/¼ pint/⅔ cup water. Stir well, bring to the boil, stirring occasionally, and simmer steadily for at least ` 10 minutes, or until the meat is hot.

STEAK BÉARNAISE

BÉARNAISE, AFTER BÉARN IN SOUTH-WEST FRANCE, IS A CREAMY EGG AND BUTTER SAUCE FLAVOURED WITH FRESH TARRAGON. IT IS A CLASSIC ACCOMPANIMENT FOR GRIDDLED, GRILLED OR PAN-FRIED STEAK AND ALSO EXCELLENT WITH ROAST BEEF. ROASTED VEGETABLES MAKE A GOOD ACCOMPANIMENT.

SERVES FOUR

INGREDIENTS
    4 sirloin steaks, each weighing about
        225g/8oz, trimmed
    15ml/1 tbsp sunflower oil (optional)
    salt and ground black pepper
For the Béarnaise sauce
    90ml/6 tbsp white wine vinegar
    12 black peppercorns
    2 bay leaves
    2 shallots, finely chopped
    4 fresh tarragon sprigs
    4 egg yolks
    225g/8oz/1 cup unsalted (sweet)
        butter, diced at room temperature
    30ml/2 tbsp chopped fresh tarragon
    freshly ground white pepper

1 Start by making the sauce. Put the vinegar, peppercorns, bay leaves, shallots and tarragon sprigs in a small pan and simmer until reduced to 30ml/2 tbsp. Strain the vinegar through a fine sieve.

2 Beat the egg yolks with salt and freshly ground white pepper in a small, heatproof bowl. Stand the bowl over a pan of very gently simmering water, then beat the strained vinegar into the yolks.

3 Gradually beat in the butter, 1 piece at a time, allowing each addition to melt before adding the next. Do not allow the water to heat beyond a gentle simmer or the sauce will overheat and curdle.

4 While cooking the sauce, heat a frying pan, griddle or grill (broiler) until hot.

COOK'S TIP
If you are confident about preparing egg and butter sauces, the best method is to reduce the flavoured vinegar before cooking the steak, then finish the sauce while the steak is cooking. This way, the sauce does not have to be kept hot and there is less risk of overheating it or allowing it to become too thick.

5 Beat the chopped fresh tarragon into the sauce and remove the pan from the heat. The sauce should be smooth, thick and glossy.

6 Cover the surface of the sauce with clear film (plastic wrap) or dampened greaseproof (waxed) paper, to prevent a skin forming, and leave over the pan of hot water – still off the heat – to keep hot while you cook the steak.

7 Season the steaks with salt and plenty freshly ground black pepper.

8 A pan is not usually oiled before cooking steak, but if it is essential to grease the pan, add only the minimum oil. Cook the steaks for 2–4 minutes on each side. The cooking time depends on the thickness of the steaks and the extent to which you want to cook them. As a guide, 2–4 minutes will give a medium-rare result.

9 Place the steaks on warmed plates. Peel the covering off the sauce and stir it lightly, then spoon it over the steaks and serve immediately.

FILLET <u>of</u> BEEF STROGANOFF

LEGEND HAS IT THAT THIS FAMOUS RUSSIAN RECIPE WAS DEVISED BY COUNT PAUL STROGANOFF'S COOK TO USE BEEF FROZEN BY THE SIBERIAN CLIMATE. THE ONLY WAY IN WHICH IT COULD BE PREPARED WAS CUT INTO VERY THIN STRIPS. THE STRIPS OF LEAN BEEF WERE SERVED IN A SOUR CREAM SAUCE FLAVOURED WITH BRANDY.

3 Add the mushrooms and stir-fry over a high heat. Transfer the vegetables and their juices to a dish, set aside.

4 Wipe the pan, then add and heat the remaining oil. Coat a batch of meat with flour, then stir-fry over a high heat until browned. Remove from the pan, then coat and stir-fry another batch. When the last batch of beef is cooked, return all the meat and vegetables to the pan. Add the brandy and simmer until it has almost evaporated.

5 Stir in the stock or consommé and seasoning and cook for 10–15 minutes, stirring frequently, or until the meat is tender and the sauce is thick and glossy. Add the sour cream and sprinkle with chopped parsley. Serve at once with rice and a simple salad.

<u>SERVES EIGHT</u>

INGREDIENTS
    1.2kg/2½lb beef fillet (tenderloin)
    30ml/2 tbsp plain (all-purpose) flour
    large pinch each of cayenne pepper
        and paprika
    75ml/5 tbsp sunflower oil
    1 large onion, chopped
    3 garlic cloves, finely chopped
    450g/1lb/6½ cups chestnut
        mushrooms, sliced
    75ml/5 tbsp brandy
    300ml/½ pint/1¼ cups beef stock
        or consommé
    300ml/½ pint/1¼ cups sour cream
    45ml/3 tbsp chopped fresh flat
        leaf parsley
    salt and ground black pepper

1 Thinly slice the fillet of beef across the grain, then cut it into fine strips. Season the flour with the cayenne pepper and paprika.

2 Heat half the oil in a large frying pan, add the onion and garlic and cook gently until the onion has softened.

COOK'S TIP
If you do not have a very large pan, it may be easier to cook the meat and vegetables in 2 separate pans. A large flameproof casserole may be used.

BEEF WELLINGTON

THIS DISH, WHICH WAS POPULAR IN THE 19TH CENTURY, IS A FILLET OF BEEF BAKED IN PUFF PASTRY.
DERIVED FROM THE CLASSIC FRENCH BOEUF EN CROÛTE, THE ENGLISH NAME WAS APPLIED TO THE
DISH IN 1815 IN HONOUR OF THE DUKE OF WELLINGTON, FOLLOWING HIS VICTORY AT THE BATTLE
OF WATERLOO. START PREPARING THE DISH WELL IN ADVANCE TO ALLOW TIME FOR THE MEAT TO
THOROUGHLY COOL BEFORE IT IS WRAPPED IN PASTRY.

SERVES SIX

INGREDIENTS
  1.5kg/3¼lb beef fillet (tenderloin)
  45ml/3 tbsp sunflower oil
  115g/4oz mushrooms, chopped
  2 garlic cloves, crushed
  175g/6oz smooth liver pâté
  30ml/2 tbsp chopped fresh parsley
  400g/14oz puff pastry, thawed if frozen
  beaten egg, to glaze
  salt and ground black pepper
  fresh flat leaf parsley, to garnish

3 Roll out the pastry into a sheet large enough to enclose the beef, plus a strip to spare. Trim off the spare pastry, then trim other edges to neaten. Spread the pâté mix down the middle of the pastry. Untie the beef and lay it on the pâté.

4 Preheat the oven to 220°C/425°F/ Gas 7. Brush the edges of the pastry with beaten egg and fold the pastry over the meat to enclose it in a neat parcel. Place the parcel on a baking sheet with the join in the pastry underneath. Cut leaf shapes from the reserved pastry. Brush the parcel with beaten egg, garnish with the pastry leaves and brush with egg. Chill for 10 minutes, or until the oven is hot.

5 Bake the Beef Wellington for 50–60 minutes, covering it loosely with foil after about 30 minutes to prevent the pastry from burning. Serve cut into thick slices garnished with parsley.

1 Preheat the oven to 220°C/425°F/ Gas 7. Tie the beef at intervals with string. Heat 30ml/2 tbsp of the oil in a large frying pan and fry the beef over a high heat for about 10 minutes, or until brown on all sides. Place in a roasting pan, bake for 20 minutes. Cool.

2 Heat the remaining oil in a frying pan and cook the mushrooms and garlic for about 5 minutes. Beat the mushroom mixture into the pâté with the parsley, season well. Set aside to cool.

STEAK, MUSHROOM <u>AND</u> ALE PIE

THIS ANGLO-IRISH DISH IS A FIRM FAVOURITE ON MENUS AT RESTAURANTS SPECIALIZING IN TRADITIONAL FARE. PIPING HOT, CREAMY MASHED POTATOES OR PARSLEY-DRESSED BOILED POTATOES AND SLIGHTLY CRUNCHY CARROTS AND GREEN BEANS OR CABBAGE ARE PERFECT ACCOMPANIMENTS; FOR A BAR-STYLE MEAL, CHIPS OR BAKED POTATOES AND A SIDE SALAD CAN BE SERVED WITH THE PIE.

SERVES FOUR

INGREDIENTS
  25g/1oz/2 tbsp butter
  1 large onion, finely chopped
  115g/4oz/1½ cups chestnut or button
    (white) mushrooms, halved
  900g/2lb lean beef in 1 piece, such
    as rump or braising steak
  30ml/2 tbsp plain (all-purpose) flour
  45ml/3 tbsp sunflower oil
  300ml/½ pint/1¼ cups stout or
    brown ale
  300ml/½ pint/1¼ cups beef stock
    or consommé
  500g/1¼lb puff pastry, thawed if frozen
  beaten egg, to glaze
  salt and ground black pepper

1 Melt the butter in a large, flameproof casserole, add the onion and cook gently, stirring occasionally, for about 5 minutes, or until it is softened but not coloured. Add the halved mushrooms and continue cooking for a further 5 minutes, stirring occasionally.

2 Meanwhile, trim the meat and cut it into 2.5cm/1in cubes. Season the flour and toss the meat in it.

COOK'S TIP
To make individual pies, divide the filling among 4 individual pie dishes. Cut the pastry into quarters and cover as above. If the dishes do not have rims, press a narrow strip of pastry around the edge of each dish to seal the lid in place. Cook as above, reducing the cooking time slightly.

3 Use a slotted spoon to remove the onion mixture from the casserole and set aside. Add and heat the oil, then brown the steak in batches over a high heat to seal in the juices.

4 Replace the vegetables, then stir in the stout or ale and stock or consommé. Bring to the boil, reduce the heat and simmer for about 1 hour, stirring occasionally, or until the meat is tender. Season to taste and transfer to a 1.5 litre/2½ pint/6¼ cup pie dish. Cover and leave to cool. If possible, chill the meat filling overnight as this allows the flavour to develop. Preheat the oven to 230°C/450°F/Gas 8.

5 Roll out the pastry in the shape of the dish and about 4cm/1½in larger all around. Cut a 2.5cm/1in strip from the edge of the pastry. Brush the rim of the dish with water and press the pastry strip on it. Brush the pastry rim with beaten egg and cover the pie with the pastry lid. Press the lid firmly in place and then trim the excess from around the edge.

6 Use the blunt edge of a knife to tap the outside edge of the pastry, pressing it down with your finger as you seal in the filling. (This technique is known as knocking up.)

7 Pinch the pastry between your fingers to flute the edge. Roll out any remaining pastry trimmings and cut out shapes to garnish the pie, brushing the shapes with a little beaten egg before pressing them lightly in place.

8 Make a hole in the middle of the pie to allow steam to escape, brush the top carefully with beaten egg and chill for 10 minutes to rest the pastry.

9 Bake the pie for 15 minutes, then reduce the oven temperature to 200°C/400°F/Gas 6 and bake for a further 15–20 minutes, or until the pastry is risen and golden.

VEAL AND HAM PIE

POPULAR FOR TWO CENTURIES, THIS CLASSIC PIE IS MOIST AND DELICIOUS. THE FLAVOURS OF THE TWO TENDER MEATS MARRY PERFECTLY IN THE DELICATE FILLING.

SERVES FOUR

INGREDIENTS

 450g/1lb boneless shoulder of
  veal, diced
 225g/8oz lean gammon (cured
  ham), diced
 15ml/1 tbsp plain (all-purpose) flour
 large pinch each of dry mustard and
  ground black pepper
 25g/1oz/2 tbsp butter
 15ml/1 tbsp sunflower oil
 1 onion, chopped
 600ml/1 pint/2½ cups chicken or
  veal stock
 2 eggs, hard-boiled (hard-cooked)
  and sliced
 30ml/2 tbsp chopped fresh parsley
For the pastry
 175g/6oz/1½ cups plain
  (all-purpose) flour
 75g/3oz/6 tbsp butter
 iced water, to mix
 beaten egg, to glaze

1 Preheat the oven to 180°C/350°F/ Gas 4. Mix the veal and gammon in a bowl. Season the flour with the mustard and pepper, then add it to the meat and toss well. Heat the butter and oil in a large, flameproof casserole, then cook the meat in batches until golden on all sides. Remove the meat from the pan.

2 Cook the onion in the fat remaining in the casserole until softened, but not coloured. Gradually stir in the stock, then replace the meat and stir well to combine. Cover and cook in the oven for 1½ hours, or until the veal is tender.

3 To make the pastry, sift the flour into a bowl and rub in the butter until the mixture resembles fine crumbs. Mix in enough iced water to bind the mixture into clumps, then press these together with your fingertips to make a dough.

4 Spoon the veal mixture into a 1.5 litre/ 2½ pint/6¼ cup pie dish. Arrange the slices of hard-boiled egg on top and sprinkle with the parsley.

5 Roll out the pastry on a lightly floured work surface to about 4cm/1½in larger than the top of the pie dish. Cut a strip from around the edge of the pastry, dampen the rim of the pie dish and press the pastry strip on it. Brush the pastry rim with beaten egg and cover it with the pastry lid.

6 Press the pastry around the rim to seal in the filling and cut off any excess. Use the blunt edge of a knife to tap the outside edge of the pastry, pressing it down with your finger as you seal in the filling. (This technique is known as knocking up.) Pinch the pastry between your fingers to flute the edge. Roll out any remaining pastry trimmings and cut out decorative shapes to garnish the top of the pie.

7 Brush the top of the pie with beaten egg and bake for 30–40 minutes, or until the pastry is well-risen and golden brown. Serve hot with slightly crunchy, steamed green cabbage and creamy mashed potato.

OSSO BUCCO <u>WITH</u> RISOTTO MILANESE

Osso bucco, literally meaning bone with a hole, is a traditional Milanese stew of veal, onions and leeks in white wine. Many of today's versions also include tomatoes. Risotto Milanese is the archetypal Italian risotto and the classic accompaniment to osso bucco.

SERVES FOUR

INGREDIENTS

50g/2oz/¼ cup butter
15ml/1 tbsp olive oil
1 large onion, chopped
1 leek, finely chopped
45ml/3 tbsp plain (all-purpose) flour
4 large portions of veal shin (shank)
600ml/1 pint/2½ cups dry white wine
salt and ground black pepper
For the risotto
25g/1oz/2 tbsp butter
1 onion, finely chopped
350g/12oz/1⅔ cups risotto rice
1 litre/1¾ pints/4 cups boiling
  chicken stock
2.5ml/½ tsp saffron threads
60ml/4 tbsp white wine
50g/2oz/⅔ cup coarsely grated
  Parmesan cheese
For the gremolata
grated rind of 1 lemon
30ml/2 tbsp chopped fresh parsley
1 garlic clove, finely chopped

1 Heat the butter and oil until sizzling in a large frying pan. Add the onion and leek, and cook gently for about 5 minutes without browning the onion. Season the flour and toss the veal in it, then add it to the pan and cook over a high heat until brown.

COOK'S TIP
When buying veal shin, ask for the pieces to be cut thickly so that they will retain the marrow during cooking – or check that they are prepared this way if purchasing pre-packed meat.

2 Gradually stir in the wine and heat until simmering. Cover the pan and simmer for 1½ hours, stirring occasionally, or until the meat is very tender. Use a slotted spoon to transfer the veal to a warm serving dish, then boil the sauce rapidly until reduced and thickened to the required consistency.

3 Make the risotto about 30 minutes before the end of the cooking time for the stew. Melt the butter in a large pan and cook the onion until softened.

4 Stir in the rice to coat all the grains in butter. Add a ladleful of boiling chicken stock and mix well. Continue adding the boiling stock a ladleful at a time, allowing each portion to be absorbed before adding the next. The whole process takes about 20 minutes.

5 Pound the saffron threads in a mortar, then stir in the wine. Add the saffron-scented wine to the risotto and cook for a final 5 minutes. Remove the pan from the heat and stir in the Parmesan.

6 Mix the lemon rind, parsley and garlic for the gremolata. Spoon some risotto on to each plate, then add some veal. Sprinkle with gremolata and serve at once.

ROAST VEAL WITH PARSLEY STUFFING

COOKING THIS JOINT OF VEAL, WITH ITS FRAGRANT PARSLEY AND LEEK STUFFING, IN A ROASTING BAG ENSURES THAT IT IS SUCCULENT AND FULL FLAVOURED WHEN SERVED.

SERVES SIX

INGREDIENTS
    25g/1oz/2 tbsp butter
    15ml/1 tbsp sunflower oil
    1 leek, finely chopped
    1 celery stick, finely chopped
    50g/2oz/1 cup fresh
      white breadcrumbs
    50g/2oz/½ cup chopped fresh flat
      leaf parsley
    900g/2lb boned loin of veal
    salt and ground black pepper

VARIATION
Other mild herbs can be used in the stuffing instead of parsley. Try tarragon, chervil and chives, but avoid strong-flavoured herbs, such as marjoram, oregano and thyme, which tend to overpower the delicate flavour of veal.

1 Preheat the oven to 180°C/350°F/Gas 4. Heat the butter and oil in a frying pan until foaming. Cook the leek and celery until they are just starting to colour, then remove the pan from the heat and stir in the breadcrumbs, parsley and seasoning.

2 Lay the joint of veal out flat. Spread the stuffing over the meat, then roll it up carefully and tie the joint at regular intervals to secure it in a neat shape.

3 Place the veal in a roasting bag and close the bag with an ovenproof tie, then place it in a roasting pan. Roast the veal for 1¼ hours.

4 Pierce the joint with a metal skewer to check whether it is cooked: when cooked the meat juices will run clear. Leave the joint to stand for 10–15 minutes, then carve it into thick slices and serve with a light gravy, sautéed potatoes and asparagus.

VEAL WITH CREAM SAUCE

THIS QUICK, EASY DINNER-PARTY DISH IS DELICIOUS SERVED WITH BUTTERED TAGLIATELLE AND LIGHTLY STEAMED GREEN VEGETABLES.

SERVES FOUR

INGREDIENTS
    15ml/1 tbsp plain (all-purpose) flour
    4 veal escalopes (veal scallops), each
      weighing 75–115g/3–4oz
    30ml/2 tbsp sunflower oil
    1 shallot, chopped
    150g/5oz/2 cups oyster
      mushrooms, sliced
    30ml/2 tbsp Marsala or
      medium-dry sherry
    200ml/7fl oz/scant 1 cup
      crème fraîche
    30ml/2 tbsp chopped fresh tarragon
    salt and ground black pepper

COOK'S TIP
If the sauce seems to be too thick, add 30ml/2 tbsp water.

1 Season the flour and use to dust the escalopes, then set aside.

2 Heat the oil in a large frying pan and cook the shallot and mushrooms for 5 minutes. Add the veal and cook over a high heat for about 1½ minutes on each side. Pour in the Marsala or sherry and cook until reduced by half.

3 Use a spatula to remove the veal from the pan. Stir the crème fraîche, tarragon and seasoning into the juices remaining in the pan and simmer very gently for 3–5 minutes, or until the sauce is thick and creamy.

4 Return the veal to the pan and heat through for 1 minute before serving.

THAI BEEF SALAD

ALL THE INGREDIENTS FOR THIS TRADITIONAL THAI DISH — KNOWN AS YAM NUA YANG — ARE WIDELY AVAILABLE IN LARGER SUPERMARKETS.

SERVES FOUR

INGREDIENTS

 675g/1½lb fillet steak (beef
  tenderloin)
 30ml/2 tbsp olive oil
 2 small mild red chillies, seeded
  and sliced
 225g/8oz/3¼ cups shiitake
  mushrooms, sliced
For the dressing
 3 spring onions (scallions),
  finely chopped
 2 garlic cloves, finely chopped
 juice of 1 lime
 15–30ml/1–2 tbsp fish or oyster
  sauce, to taste
 5ml/1 tsp soft light brown sugar
 30ml/2 tbsp chopped fresh
  coriander (cilantro)
To serve
 1 cos or romaine lettuce, torn
  into strips
 175g/6oz cherry tomatoes, halved
 5cm/2in piece cucumber, peeled,
  halved and thinly sliced
 45ml/3 tbsp toasted sesame seeds

1 Preheat the grill (broiler) until hot, then cook the steak for 2–4 minutes on each side depending on your taste. Leave to cool for at least 15 minutes.

2 Use a very sharp knife to slice the meat as thinly as possible and place the slices in a bowl.

VARIATION
If you can find them, yellow chillies make a colourful addition to this dish. Substitute one for one of the red chillies.

3 Heat the olive oil in a small frying pan. Add the seeded and sliced red chillies and the sliced mushrooms and cook for 5 minutes, stirring occasionally. Turn off the heat and add the grilled (broiled) steak slices to the pan, then stir well to coat the beef slices in the chilli and mushroom mixture.

4 Stir all the ingredients for the dressing together, then pour it over the meat mixture and toss gently.

5 Arrange the salad ingredients on a serving plate. Spoon the warm steak mixture in the centre and sprinkle the sesame seeds over. Serve at once.

CHILLI CON CARNE

ORIGINALLY MADE WITH FINELY CHOPPED BEEF, CHILLIES AND KIDNEY BEANS BY HUNGRY LABOURERS WORKING ON THE TEXAN RAILROAD, THIS FAMOUS TEX-MEX STEW HAS BECOME AN INTERNATIONAL FAVOURITE. SERVE WITH RICE OR BAKED POTATOES TO COMPLETE THIS HEARTY MEAL.

SERVES EIGHT

INGREDIENTS

1.2kg/2½lb lean braising steak
30ml/2 tbsp sunflower oil
1 large onion, chopped
2 garlic cloves, finely chopped
15ml/1 tbsp plain (all-purpose) flour
300ml/½ pint/1¼ cups red wine
300ml/½ pint/1¼ cups beef stock
30ml/2 tbsp tomato purée (paste)
fresh coriander (cilantro) leaves,
  to garnish
salt and ground black pepper
For the beans
30ml/2 tbsp olive oil
1 onion, chopped
1 red chilli, seeded and chopped
2 x 400g/14oz cans red kidney
  beans, drained and rinsed
400g/14oz can chopped tomatoes
For the topping
6 tomatoes, peeled and chopped
1 green chilli, seeded and chopped
30ml/2 tbsp chopped fresh chives
30ml/2 tbsp chopped fresh
  coriander (cilantro)
150ml/¼ pint/⅔ cup sour cream

1 Cut the meat into thick strips and then cut it crossways into small cubes. Heat the oil in a large, flameproof casserole. Add the onion and garlic, and cook until softened but not coloured. Meanwhile, season the flour and toss a batch of meat in it.

VARIATION
This stew is equally good served with warm tortillas instead of rice.

2 Use a slotted spoon to remove the onion from the pan, then add the floured beef and cook over a high heat until browned on all sides. Remove from the pan and set aside, then flour and brown another batch of meat.

3 When the last batch of meat is browned, return the first batches with the onion to the pan. Stir in the wine, stock and tomato purée. Bring to the boil, reduce the heat and simmer for 45 minutes, or until tender.

4 Meanwhile, for the beans, heat the olive oil in a frying pan and cook the onion and chilli until softened. Add the kidney beans and tomatoes and simmer gently for 20–25 minutes, or until thickened and reduced.

5 Mix the tomatoes, chilli, chives and coriander for the topping. Ladle the meat mixture on to warmed plates. Add a layer of bean mixture and tomato topping. Finish with sour cream and garnish with coriander.

CHUNKY BURGERS WITH SPICY RELISH

BURGERS ARE EASY TO MAKE AND THESE TASTE TERRIFIC — FAR BETTER THAN ANY YOU CAN BUY.
USE LEAN BEEF SO THAT THE BURGERS ARE NOT FATTY.

SERVES FOUR

INGREDIENTS
    450g/1lb lean minced (ground) beef
    1 shallot, chopped
    30ml/2 tbsp chopped fresh flat
        leaf parsley
    30ml/2 tbsp tomato ketchup
    salt and ground black pepper
For the spicy relish
    15ml/1 tbsp olive oil
    1 shallot, chopped
    1 garlic clove, crushed
    1 small green chilli, seeded and
        finely chopped
    400g/14oz can ratatouille
To serve
    4 burger buns
    1 Little Gem (Bibb) lettuce heart,
        separated into leaves

1 Mix the minced beef, shallot, chopped fresh flat leaf parsley, ketchup and seasoning in a mixing bowl until thoroughly combined. Divide the mixture into quarters and shape into four chunky burgers, pressing them firmly between the palms of your hands. Place the burgers on a plate and set aside until ready to cook.

2 To make the spicy relish, heat the olive oil in a frying pan and cook the shallot, garlic and chilli for a few minutes, stirring, until softened. Stir in the ratatouille and simmer for 5 minutes.

3 Meanwhile, preheat the grill (broiler), a griddle or frying pan. Grill (broil) or fry the burgers for about 5 minutes on each side, or until cooked through.

4 Split the burger buns and toast them, if you like. Arrange a few lettuce leaves on the bun bases, then top with the burgers and add a little of the warm spicy relish. Add the bun tops and serve at once, offering the remaining relish and any extra lettuce leaves separately. Serve with chunky chips (French fries) or baked potatoes.

ITALIAN MEATBALLS

SUCCULENT MEATBALLS IN A COLOURFUL PEPPER SAUCE ARE DELICIOUS WITH RICE OR PASTA, AND
THEY ARE ALWAYS A HIT WITH CHILDREN AS WELL AS ADULTS.

SERVES FOUR

INGREDIENTS
    10ml/2 tsp sunflower oil
    1 shallot, chopped
    2 garlic cloves, finely chopped
    15ml/1 tbsp fresh thyme leaves
    675g/1½lb minced (ground) beef
    1 slice white bread, crust removed,
        reduced to crumbs
    1 egg
    salt and ground black pepper
    fresh thyme leaves, to garnish
For the sauce
    3 red (bell) peppers, halved
        and seeded
    1 onion, quartered
    400g/14oz can chopped tomatoes

1 Heat the oil in a frying pan and cook the shallot and garlic for 5 minutes, or until softened. Remove from the heat, add the thyme, then turn into a bowl.

2 Add the minced beef, breadcrumbs, egg and seasoning to the shallot mixture. Mix until all the ingredients are thoroughly combined. Using your hands, shape the mixture into 20 small meatballs, then chill them until the sauce is ready.

3 To make the sauce, preheat the grill (broiler). Arrange the peppers on the grilling rack with the pieces of onion. Grill (broil) for 12–15 minutes, turning frequently, or until the pepper skins are blackened. Remove from under the heat, cover the peppers with a large dishtowel and leave until cool enough to handle.

4 Peel the peppers and place them in a blender or food processor with the grilled (broiled) onion and the tomatoes. Process until smooth, then add seasoning to taste.

5 Cook the meatballs in a large, non-stick frying pan for about 10–15 minutes, gently rolling them around to brown them evenly all over.

6 Add the puréed pepper and tomato mixture and bring to the boil, then simmer for 10 minutes. Transfer to a dish and scatter with thyme leaves to garnish, then serve at once.

LAMB DISHES

Naturally tender, succulent and full of flavour, lamb is one of the truly international meats and is cooked in almost every country — a fact reflected in this eclectic range of recipes, which includes Moussaka, a dish made in both Greece and Turkey, Spiced Lamb with Tomatoes and Peppers from India, and the North African classic, Tagine of Lamb with Couscous. There are western European and American favourites, such as Roast Leg of Lamb, and traditional recipes with an enticing, contemporary twist, such as Redcurrant-glazed Lamb Chops with Celeriac and Thyme Mash, and Braised Shoulder of Lamb with Pearl Barley and Baby Vegetables.

ROAST LEG OF LAMB

WHEN YOUNG LAMB WAS SEASONAL TO SPRINGTIME, A ROAST LEG WAS AN EASTER SPECIALITY, SERVED WITH A SAUCE USING THE FIRST SPRIGS OF MINT OF THE YEAR AND EARLY NEW POTATOES. ROAST LAMB IS NOW WELL ESTABLISHED AS A YEAR-ROUND FAMILY FAVOURITE FOR SUNDAY LUNCH, OFTEN SERVED WITH CRISP ROAST POTATOES.

SERVES SIX

INGREDIENTS
  1.5kg/3¼lb leg of lamb
  4 garlic cloves, sliced
  2 fresh rosemary sprigs
  30ml/2 tbsp light olive oil
  300ml/½ pint/1¼ cups red wine
  5ml/1 tsp clear honey
  45ml/3 tbsp redcurrant jelly
  salt and ground black pepper
For the roast potatoes
  45ml/3 tbsp white vegetable fat or
    lard (shortening)
  1.3kg/3lb potatoes, such as Desirée,
    cut into chunks
For the mint sauce
  about 15g/½oz/½ cup fresh mint
  10ml/2 tsp caster (superfine) sugar
  15ml/1 tbsp boiling water
  30ml/2 tbsp white wine vinegar

1 Preheat the oven to 220°C/425°F/Gas 7. Make small slits into the lamb all over the joint. Press a slice of garlic and a few rosemary leaves into each slit, then place the joint in a roasting pan and season well. Drizzle the oil over the lamb and roast the joint for about 1 hour.

COOK'S TIP
To make a quick and tasty gravy from the pan juices, add about 300ml/½ pint/1¼ cups red wine, stock or water and boil, stirring occasionally, until reduced and well-flavoured. Season to taste, then strain into a sauce boat to serve.

2 Meanwhile, mix the wine, honey and redcurrant jelly in a small pan and heat, stirring, until the jelly melts. Bring to the boil, then reduce the heat and simmer until reduced by half. Spoon this glaze over the lamb and return it to the oven for 30–45 minutes.

3 To prepare the potatoes, put the fat in a roasting pan on the oven shelf above the meat. Boil the potatoes for 5–10 minutes, then drain them and fluff up the surface of each with a fork.

4 Add the prepared potatoes to the hot fat and baste well, then roast them for 40–50 minutes, or until they are crisp.

5 Make the mint sauce while the potatoes are roasting. Place the mint on a chopping board and sprinkle the sugar over the top. Chop finely, then transfer the mint and sugar to a bowl.

6 Add the boiling water and stir until the sugar has dissolved. Add 15ml/1 tbsp vinegar and taste the sauce before adding the remaining vinegar. You may want to add slightly less or more than the suggested quantity. Leave the mint sauce to stand until you are ready to serve the meal.

7 Cover the lamb with foil and set it aside in a warm place to rest for 10–15 minutes before carving. Serve with the crisp roast potatoes, mint sauce and a selection of seasonal vegetables.

HERB-CRUSTED RACK OF LAMB
WITH PUY LENTILS

THIS ROAST IS QUICK AND EASY TO PREPARE, YET IMPRESSIVE WHEN SERVED: THE PERFECT CHOICE WHEN ENTERTAINING. BOILED OR STEAMED NEW POTATOES AND LIGHTLY COOKED BROCCOLI OR SUGAR SNAP PEAS ARE SUITABLE ACCOMPANIMENTS FOR THE LAMB. SERVE WITH A LIGHT RED WINE.

SERVES FOUR

INGREDIENTS

    2 x 6-bone racks of lamb, chined
    50g/2oz/1 cup fresh white
      breadcrumbs
    2 large garlic cloves, crushed
    90ml/6 tbsp chopped mixed fresh
      herbs, such as rosemary, thyme, flat
      leaf parsley and marjoram, plus
      extra sprigs to garnish
    50g/2oz/¼ cup butter, melted
    salt and ground black pepper
For the Puy lentils
    1 red onion, chopped
    30ml/2 tbsp olive oil
    400g/14oz can Puy or green lentils,
      rinsed and drained
    400g/14oz can chopped tomatoes
    30ml/2 tbsp chopped fresh parsley

1 Preheat the oven to 220°C/425°F/ Gas 7. Trim any excess fat from the lamb, season well with salt and pepper.

2 Mix the breadcrumbs, garlic, herbs and butter, and press on to the fat-sides of the lamb. Place in a roasting pan and roast for 25 minutes. Cover; stand for 5 minutes before carving.

3 Cook the onion in the olive oil until softened. Add the lentils and tomatoes and cook gently for 5 minutes, or until the lentils are piping hot. Stir in the parsley and season to taste.

4 Cut each rack of lamb in half and serve with the lentils and new potatoes. Garnish with herb sprigs.

BRAISED SHOULDER OF LAMB WITH PEARL BARLEY AND BABY VEGETABLES

PEARL BARLEY ABSORBS ALL THE WONDERFUL MEAT JUICES AND STOCK TO BECOME FULL-FLAVOURED AND NUTTY IN TEXTURE WHEN COOKED.

SERVES FOUR

INGREDIENTS
   60ml/4 tbsp olive oil
   1 large onion, chopped
   2 garlic cloves, chopped
   2 celery sticks, sliced
   a little plain (all-purpose) flour
   675g/1½lb boned shoulder of lamb,
      cut into cubes
   900ml–1 litre/1½–1¾ pints/
      3¾–4 cups lamb stock
   115g/4oz pearl barley
   225g/8oz baby carrots
   225g/8oz baby turnips
   salt and ground black pepper
   30ml/2 tbsp chopped fresh marjoram,
      to garnish

1 Heat 45ml/3 tbsp of the oil in a flameproof casserole. Cook the onion and garlic until softened, add the celery, then cook until the vegetables brown.

2 Season the flour and toss the lamb in it. Use a slotted spoon to remove the vegetables from the casserole. Add and heat the remaining oil with the juices in the casserole. Brown the lamb in batches until golden.

3 When all the meat is browned, return it to the casserole with the vegetables. Stir in 900ml/1½ pints/3¾ cups of the stock and the pearl barley. Cover, then bring to the boil, reduce the heat and simmer for 1 hour, or until the pearl barley and lamb are tender.

4 Add the baby carrots and turnips to the casserole for the final 15 minutes cooking. Stir the meat occasionally during cooking and add the remaining stock, if necessary. Stir in seasoning to taste, and serve piping hot, garnished with marjoram. Warm, crusty bread would make a good accompaniment.

REDCURRANT-GLAZED LAMB CHOPS
WITH CELERIAC AND THYME MASH

THIS IS A BRILLIANT SUPPER DISH TO LIFT THE SPIRITS ON A COLD WINTER'S EVENING. THE REDCURRANT GLAZE HELPS TO SEAL THE JUICES INTO THE MEAT AND IT COMPLEMENTS THE FLAVOUR OF THE LAMB TO PERFECTION.

SERVES FOUR

INGREDIENTS
  30ml/2 tbsp redcurrant jelly
  30ml/2 tbsp mint jelly
  grated rind and juice of
    1 orange
  12 lamb cutlets (rib chops),
    trimmed
  fresh rosemary, to garnish
For the celeriac mash
  675g/1½lb celeriac, diced
  675g/1½lb potatoes, diced
  25g/1oz/2 tbsp butter
  30ml/2 tbsp double (heavy) cream
  15ml/1 tbsp fresh thyme leaves
  salt and ground black pepper

VARIATION
To make a more colourful vegetable mash, use sweet potatoes or carrots in place of the celeriac.

1 First prepare the mash. Cook the celeriac and potatoes in boiling salted water for 20 minutes, or until tender. Drain well, then add the butter, cream and thyme. Mash the vegetables and season to taste.

2 Heat the jellies with the orange rind and juice in a small pan, stirring occasionally until smooth. Bring to the boil and cook until reduced by half.

3 Arrange the lamb cutlets on a hot griddle pan and season them well. Drizzle half the redcurrant and mint glaze over the cutlets and then cook for 3–5 minutes. Turn the cutlets and pour the remaining glaze over them. Cook for a further 3–5 minutes.

4 Garnish the cutlets with rosemary and serve at once, with the celeriac and thyme mash.

BARBECUED LAMB STEAKS
WITH RED PEPPER SALSA

VIBRANT RED PEPPER SALSA BRINGS OUT THE BEST IN SUCCULENT LAMB STEAKS TO MAKE A DISH THAT LOOKS AS GOOD AS IT TASTES. SERVE WITH A SELECTION OF SALADS AND CRUSTY BREAD.

SERVES SIX

INGREDIENTS
  6 lamb steaks
  about 15g/½oz fresh
    rosemary leaves
  2 garlic cloves, sliced
  60ml/4 tbsp olive oil
  30ml/2 tbsp maple syrup
  salt and ground black pepper
For the salsa
  200g/7oz red (bell) peppers, roasted,
    peeled, seeded and chopped
  1 plump garlic clove,
    finely chopped
  15ml/1 tbsp chopped chives
  30ml/2 tbsp extra virgin olive oil
  fresh flat leaf parsley, to garnish

1 Place the lamb steaks in a dish and season with salt and pepper. Pull the leaves off the rosemary and sprinkle them over the meat. Add the slices of garlic cloves, then drizzle the oil and maple syrup over the top. Cover and chill until ready to cook. The lamb can be left to marinate in the refrigerator for up to 24 hours.

2 Make sure the steaks are liberally coated with the marinating ingredients, then grill them over a hot barbecue for 2–5 minutes on each side. The cooking time depends on the heat of the barbecue coals and the thickness of the steaks as well as the result required – rare, medium or well cooked.

3 While the lamb steaks are cooking, mix together all the ingredients for the salsa. Serve the barbecued lamb steaks freshly cooked, and offer the salsa separately or spoon it on to the plates with the meat. Garnish with sprigs of flat leaf parsley.

MOUSSAKA

THIS IS A TRADITIONAL EASTERN MEDITERRANEAN DISH, POPULAR IN BOTH GREECE AND TURKEY.
LAYERS OF LAMB, AUBERGINES, TOMATOES AND ONIONS ARE TOPPED WITH A CREAMY YOGURT AND
CHEESE SAUCE IN THIS DELICIOUS, AUTHENTIC RECIPE.

SERVES FOUR

INGREDIENTS
    450g/1lb aubergines (eggplant)
    150ml/¼ pint/⅔ cup olive oil
    1 large onion, chopped
    2–3 garlic cloves, finely chopped
    675g/1½lb minced (ground) lamb
    15ml/1 tbsp plain (all-purpose) flour
    400g/14oz can chopped tomatoes
    30ml/2 tbsp chopped mixed fresh
        herbs, such as parsley and oregano
    salt and ground black pepper
For the topping
    300ml/½ pint/1¼ cups natural
        (plain) yogurt
    2 eggs
    25g/1oz feta cheese, crumbled
    25g/1oz/⅓ cup freshly grated
        Parmesan cheese

1 Cut the aubergines into thin slices and place them in a colander, sprinkling each layer with salt.

2 Cover the aubergines with a plate and a weight, then leave to drain for about 30 minutes. Drain and rinse well, then pat dry with kitchen paper.

3 Heat 45ml/3 tbsp of the oil in a large, heavy pan. Fry the onion and garlic until softened, but not coloured. Add the lamb and cook over a high heat, stirring often, until browned.

4 Stir in the flour until mixed, then stir in the tomatoes, herbs and seasoning. Bring to the boil, reduce the heat and simmer gently for 20 minutes.

5 Meanwhile, heat a little of the remaining oil in a large frying pan. Add as many aubergine slices as can be laid evenly in the pan, then cook until golden on both sides. Set the cooked slices aside. Heat more oil and continue frying the aubergines in batches, adding oil as necessary.

COOK'S TIP
Aubergines that are available today do not taste bitter; therefore it is not usually necessary to salt them before cooking. However if they are to be fried, as in this recipe, salting and drying them reduces the amount of fat that they absorb and helps them to brown.

6 Preheat the oven to 180°C/350°F/ Gas 4. Using a spatula, arrange half the aubergine slices in a large, shallow ovenproof dish.

7 Top with about half of the meat and tomato mixture, then add the remaining aubergine slices. Finally, spread the remaining meat mixture over the top.

8 Beat together the yogurt and eggs, then mix in the feta and Parmesan cheeses, pour the mixture over the meat and spread it evenly.

9 Transfer the moussaka to the oven and bake for 35–40 minutes, or until golden and bubbling. Serve with a simple, mixed leaf, green salad.

VARIATION
Use large courgettes (zucchini) in place of the aubergines, if you like, and cut them diagonally into fairly thick slices. There is no need to salt the courgettes before frying them.

SPICED LAMB WITH TOMATOES AND PEPPERS

*SELECT LEAN TENDER LAMB FROM THE LEG FOR THIS LIGHTLY SPICED CURRY WITH SUCCULENT
PEPPERS AND WEDGES OF ONION. SERVE WARM NAAN BREAD TO MOP UP THE TOMATO-RICH JUICES.*

SERVES SIX

INGREDIENTS

    1.5kg/3¼lb boneless lamb, cubed
    250ml/8fl oz/1 cup natural
      (plain) yogurt
    30ml/2 tbsp sunflower oil
    3 onions
    2 red (bell) peppers, cut into chunks
    3 garlic cloves, finely chopped
    1 red chilli, seeded and chopped
    2.5cm/1in piece fresh root ginger,
      peeled and chopped
    30ml/2 tbsp mild curry paste
    2 x 400g/14oz cans chopped
      tomatoes
    large pinch of saffron threads
    800g/1¾lb plum tomatoes, halved,
      seeded and cut into chunks
    salt and ground black pepper
    chopped fresh coriander (cilantro),
      to garnish

1 Mix the lamb with the yogurt in a
bowl. Cover and chill for about 1 hour.
Marinating in yogurt helps to tenderize
the meat and reduce the cooking time.

2 Heat the oil in a karahi, wok or large
pan. Drain the lamb and reserve the
yogurt, then cook the lamb in batches
until it is golden on all sides – this takes
about 15 minutes in total. Remove from
the pan and set aside.

3 Cut 2 of the onions into wedges
(6 from each onion) and add to the oil
remaining in the pan. Fry the onion
wedges over a medium heat for about
10 minutes, or until they are beginning
to colour. Add the peppers and cook for
a further 5 minutes. Use a slotted
spoon to remove the vegetables from
the pan and set aside.

4 Meanwhile, chop the remaining onion.
Add it to the oil remaining in the pan
with the garlic, chilli and ginger, and
cook, stirring often, until softened.

5 Stir in the curry paste and canned
tomatoes with the reserved yogurt
marinade. Replace the lamb, add
seasoning to taste and stir well. Bring to
the boil, reduce the heat and simmer
for about 30 minutes.

6 Pound the saffron to a powder in a
mortar, stir in a little boiling water to
dissolve the saffron. Add this liquid to
the curry. Replace the onion and pepper
mixture. Stir in the fresh tomatoes and
bring back to simmering point, then
cook for 15 minutes. Garnish with
sprigs of fresh coriander.

TAGINE OF LAMB WITH COUSCOUS

A TAGINE IS A CLASSIC MOROCCAN STEW AND IT IS ALSO THE NAME GIVEN TO THE EARTHENWARE POT WITH A CONICAL LID IN WHICH THE STEW IS COOKED. COUSCOUS HAS TWO MEANINGS AND REFERS TO A FINISHED DISH AS WELL AS AN INGREDIENT. FROM THE ARABIC KUSKUS, THE TITLE IS GIVEN TO THE POPULAR NORTH AFRICAN STEW OF MEAT — OR CHICKEN — AND VEGETABLES IN A THIN, YET FULL-FLAVOURED AND SPICY, SAUCE SERVED ON COUSCOUS, THE CRACKED WHEAT PRODUCT THAT IS NOW WIDELY AVAILABLE IN INSTANT, PRE-COOKED FORM.

SERVES SIX

INGREDIENTS

- 1kg/2¼lb lean boneless lamb, such as shoulder or neck fillet
- 25g/1oz/2 tbsp butter
- 15ml/1 tbsp sunflower oil
- 1 large onion, chopped
- 2 garlic cloves, chopped
- 2.5cm/1in piece fresh root ginger, peeled and finely chopped
- 1 red (bell) pepper, seeded and chopped
- 900ml/1½ pints/3¾ cups lamb stock or water
- 250g/9oz ready-to-eat prunes
- juice of 1 lemon
- 15ml/1 tbsp clear honey
- 1.5ml/¼ tsp saffron threads
- 1 cinnamon stick, broken in half
- 50g/2oz/½ cup flaked (sliced) almonds, toasted
- salt and ground black pepper

To serve

- 450g/1lb/2½ cups couscous
- 25g/1oz/2 tbsp butter
- 30ml/2 tbsp chopped fresh coriander (cilantro)

3 Meanwhile, cook the couscous according to packet instructions, usually by placing in a large bowl and pouring in boiling water to cover the "grains" by 2.5cm/1in. Stir well, then cover and leave to stand for 5–10 minutes. The couscous absorbs the water and swells to become tender and fluffy. Stir in the butter, chopped fresh coriander and seasoning to taste.

1 Trim the lamb and cut it into 2.5cm/1in cubes. Heat the butter and oil in a large flameproof casserole until foaming. Add the onion, garlic and ginger and cook, stirring occasionally, until softened but not coloured. Add the lamb and red pepper and mix well. Pour in the stock or water.

2 Add the prunes, lemon juice, honey, saffron threads and cinnamon. Season with salt and pepper and stir well. Bring to the boil, then reduce the heat and cover the casserole. Simmer for 1½–2 hours, stirring occasionally, or until the meat is melt-in-the-mouth tender.

4 Taste the stew for seasoning and add more salt and pepper if necessary. Pile the couscous into a large, warmed serving dish or on to individual warmed bowls or plates. Ladle the stew on to the couscous and sprinkle the toasted flaked almonds over the top.

LAMB STEW <u>WITH</u> BABY ONIONS <u>AND</u> NEW POTATOES

THIS FRESH LEMON-SEASONED STEW IS FINISHED WITH AN ITALIAN MIXTURE OF CHOPPED GARLIC, PARSLEY AND LEMON RIND KNOWN AS GREMOLATA, THE TRADITIONAL TOPPING FOR OSSO BUCCO.

SERVES SIX

INGREDIENTS

1kg/2¼lb boneless shoulder of lamb, trimmed of fat and cut into 5cm/ 2in cubes
1 garlic clove, finely chopped
finely grated rind of ½ lemon and juice of 1 lemon
90ml/6 tbsp olive oil
45ml/3 tbsp plain (all-purpose) flour
1 large onion, sliced
5 anchovy fillets in olive oil, drained
2.5ml/½ tsp caster (superfine) sugar
300ml/1¼ pint/1¼ cups white wine
475ml/16fl oz/2 cups lamb stock or half stock and half water
1 fresh bay leaf
fresh thyme sprig
fresh parsley sprig
500g/1¼lb small new potatoes
250g/9oz shallots, peeled but left whole
45ml/3 tbsp double (heavy) cream (optional)
salt and ground black pepper
For the gremolata
1 garlic clove, finely chopped
finely shredded rind of ½ lemon
45ml/3 tbsp chopped fresh flat leaf parsley

1 Mix the lamb with the garlic and the rind and juice of ½ lemon. Season with pepper and mix in 15ml/1 tbsp olive oil. Leave to marinate for 12–24 hours.

2 Drain the lamb, reserving the marinade, and pat the lamb dry with kitchen paper. Preheat the oven to 180°C/350°F/Gas 4.

COOK'S TIP
A mezzaluna (double-handled, half-moon shaped, curved chopping blade) makes a very good job of chopping gremolata ingredients. If using a food processor or electric chopper, take care not to overprocess the mixture as it is easy to mince the ingredients to a paste.

3 Heat 30ml/2 tbsp olive oil in a large frying pan. Season the flour with salt and pepper and toss the lamb in it to coat, shaking off any excess. Seal the lamb well on all sides in the hot oil. Do this in batches, transferring each batch of lamb to a flameproof casserole as you brown it. You may need to add an extra 15ml/1 tbsp olive oil to the pan as you proceed.

4 Reduce the heat, add another 15ml/ 1 tbsp oil to the pan and cook the onion gently over a very low heat, stirring frequently for 10 minutes, until softened and golden but not browned. Add the anchovies and caster sugar and cook, mashing the anchovies into the soft onion with a wooden spoon.

5 Add the reserved marinade, increase the heat a little and cook for about 1–2 minutes, then pour in the wine and stock or stock and water, and bring to the boil. Simmer gently for about 5 minutes, then pour over the lamb.

6 Tie the bay leaf, thyme and parsley together and add to the lamb. Season with salt and pepper, then cover tightly and cook in the oven for 1 hour. Stir the potatoes into the casserole and cook for a further 20 minutes.

7 Meanwhile, to make the gremolata, chop all the ingredients together finely. Place in a dish, cover and set aside.

8 Heat the remaining oil in a frying pan and brown the shallots on all sides, then stir them into the lamb. Cover and cook for a further 30–40 minutes, until the lamb is tender. Transfer the lamb and vegetables to a dish and keep warm. Discard the herbs.

9 Boil the cooking juices to reduce and concentrate them, then add the cream, if using, and simmer for 2–3 minutes. Adjust the seasoning, adding a little lemon juice to taste. Pour this sauce over the lamb, sprinkle the gremolata on top and serve immediately.

L A M B A N D G I N G E R S T I R - F R Y W I T H E G G N O O D L E S

STIR-FRYING IS A TRADITIONAL ASIAN TECHNIQUE; IT CAN ALSO BE ONE OF THE QUICKEST, EASIEST AND HEALTHIEST COOKING METHODS. A WOK IS THE CLASSIC PAN, BUT A LARGE FRYING PAN, WITH SIDES THAT ARE DEEPER THAN USUAL, CAN BE USED, OR EVEN A LARGE PAN IS SUITABLE — IT IS IMPORTANT TO HAVE PLENTY OF SPACE FOR TOSSING AND TURNING INGREDIENTS.

SERVES FOUR

INGREDIENTS
  45ml/3 tbsp sesame oil
  3 spring onions (scallions), sliced
  2 garlic cloves, crushed
  2.5cm/1in piece fresh root ginger,
    peeled and finely sliced
  1 red chilli, seeded and finely sliced
  1 red (bell) pepper, halved, seeded
    and sliced
  450g/1lb lean boneless lamb, cut
    into fine strips
  115g/4oz/1½ cups fresh shiitake
    mushrooms, sliced
  2 carrots, cut into matchstick strips
  300g/11oz fresh Chinese egg noodles
  300g/11oz pak choi (bok
    choy), shredded

1 Heat half the oil in a wok or large frying pan. Stir-fry the spring onions and garlic for 5 minutes, or until golden. Add the ginger, chilli and pepper and continue stir-frying for 5 minutes, until the chilli and pepper start to soften. Use a draining spoon to remove the cooked vegetables.

2 Add the remaining oil and stir-fry the lamb in batches until golden. Add the mushrooms and carrots and stir-fry for 2–3 minutes. Remove from the wok and set aside with the pepper mixture. Stir-fry the noodles and pak choi for about 5 minutes.

3 Finally, replace all the cooked ingredients and stir-fry for a couple of minutes or until the mixture is heated through. Serve at once, offering soy sauce to season at the table.

COOK'S TIP
If fresh egg noodles are not available, use the dried type. Cook them according to the packet instructions, drain and rinse under cold water, then drain well.

I T A L I A N B R A I S E D S H A N K S W I T H R A T A T O U I L L E

FOR THIS MODERN MEDITERRANEAN MEAL, LAMB SHANKS ARE BRAISED IN ITALIAN STYLE WITH RATATOUILLE: A DISH OF MIXED VEGETABLES SIMMERED IN OLIVE OIL.

SERVES FOUR

INGREDIENTS
  4 lamb shanks
  45ml/3 tbsp olive oil
  1 large red onion, finely chopped
  2 large garlic cloves,
    finely chopped
  1 large aubergine (eggplant), diced
  3 courgettes (zucchini), diced
  2 x 400g/14oz cans chopped
    tomatoes
  300ml/½ pint/1¼ cups well-
    flavoured lamb stock
  400g/14oz can flageolet (small
    cannellini) beans, rinsed
    and drained
  15ml/1 tbsp chopped fresh oregano
  15ml/1 tbsp chopped fresh rosemary
  5ml/1 tsp clear honey
  salt and ground black pepper

1 Season the lamb shanks with salt and ground black pepper. Heat the oil in a large flameproof casserole and fry the shanks until golden on all sides, then remove from the pan and set aside.

2 Add the onion and garlic and cook gently until the onion is softened. Add the diced aubergine and courgettes and cook the vegetable mixture for a further 5 minutes.

3 Stir in the tomatoes and stock, then nestle the lamb shanks back into the vegetable mixture. Bring to the boil, reduce the heat and cover the casserole. Simmer for about 1 hour.

4 Remove the lamb. Stir the beans into the vegetables with the herbs and honey, and simmer, covered, for about 45 minutes more, topping up with stock if necessary. Replace the lamb 10 minutes from the end of cooking to heat through. Serve with mashed potatoes or couscous.

COOK'S TIP
Butchers are usually happy to supply less-popular cuts, such as lamb shanks, given a couple of days' notice, so remember to order them in advance. Alternatively, use lamb chump chops or neck of lamb (neck slices).

PORK, BACON AND HAM DISHES

As the food of commoners rather than kings, pork, bacon and ham have, over the centuries, been taken for granted. That's a shame, because these are extremely tasty meats — as perfect for quick meals as for slow-cooked roasts. Traditional recipes such as Somerset Cider-glazed Ham or the French classic, Pork and Bacon Rillettes with Onion Salad will reward the time spent in the kitchen. Others, such as creamy Carbonara Abruzzi or Stir-fried Pork with Mushrooms, are quick to cook and ideal for midweek meals, while delicious Muffins with Bacon, Eggs and Quick Hollandaise Sauce can be served at any time of the day — or night.

STUFFED ROAST LOIN OF PORK WITH APPLE SAUCE

ROASTS MAKE GREAT SUNDAY LUNCHES BECAUSE THEY REQUIRE MINIMUM ATTENTION ONCE THEY ARE IN THE OVEN, SO THE COOK CAN RELAX WITH THE FAMILY OR FRIENDS.

SERVES SIX

INGREDIENTS

15ml/1 tbsp light olive oil
2 leeks, chopped
150g/5oz/⅔ cup ready-to-eat dried
   apricots, chopped
150g/5oz/1 cup dried dates, stoned
   (pitted) and chopped
75g/3oz/1½ cups fresh white
   breadcrumbs
2 eggs, beaten
15ml/1 tbsp fresh thyme leaves
1.5kg/3¼lb boned loin of pork
salt and ground black pepper
For the apple sauce
   450g/1lb cooking apples
   30ml/2 tbsp (hard) cider or water
   25g/1oz/2 tbsp butter
   30 ml/2 tbsp caster (superfine) sugar

1 Preheat oven to 220°C/425°F/Gas 7. Heat the oil in a large pan and cook the leeks until softened. Stir in the apricots, dates, breadcrumbs, eggs and thyme, and season with salt and pepper.

2 Lay the pork skin-side up, and use a sharp knife to score the rind crossways.

3 Turn the meat over and cut down the centre of the joint to within 1cm/½in of the rind and fat, then work from the middle outwards towards one side, cutting most of the meat off the rind, keeping a 1cm/½in layer of meat on top of the rind. Cut to within 2.5cm/1in of the side of the joint. Repeat on the other side of the joint.

4 Spoon half the stuffing over the joint, then fold the meat over it.

5 Tie the joint back into its original shape, then place in a roasting pan and rub the skin with salt. Roast for about 40 minutes, then reduce the oven temperature to 190°C/375°F/Gas 5 and cook for a further 1½ hours, or until the meat is tender and cooked through.

6 When cooked, cover the meat closely with foil and leave to stand in a warm place for 10 minutes before carving.

COOK'S TIP
The resting time before carving is very important, so don't be tempted to skip it.

7 Meanwhile, shape the remaining stuffing into walnut-size balls. Arrange on a tray, cover with clear film (plastic wrap) and chill until 20 minutes before the pork is cooked. Then add the stuffing balls to the roasting pan and baste them with the cooking juices.

8 To make the apple sauce, peel, core and chop the apples, then place in a small pan with the cider or water and cook for 5–10 minutes, stirring occasionally, until very soft. Beat well or process in a blender or food processor to make smooth apple sauce. Beat in the butter and sugar, adding a little more sugar to taste, if required. Reheat the apple sauce just before serving, if necessary.

9 Carve the joint into thick slices. If the crackling is very hard, you may find it is easier to slice the crackling off the joint first, before carving the meat, then cut the crackling into serving pieces using poultry shears or a heavy, sharp chef's knife or cleaver. Serve the pork with the crackling, stuffing balls, apple sauce and a selection of seasonal vegetables.

SOMERSET CIDER-GLAZED HAM

WILLIAM THE CONQUEROR INTRODUCED CIDER-MAKING TO ENGLAND FROM NORMANDY IN 1066. THIS WONDERFUL OLD WEST-COUNTRY JOINT GLAZED WITH CIDER IS TRADITIONALLY SERVED WITH CRANBERRY SAUCE AND IS IDEAL FOR CHRISTMAS OR BOXING DAY.

SERVES EIGHT TO TEN

INGREDIENTS
   2kg/4½lb middle gammon (cured
    ham) joint
   1.3 litres/2¼ pints/5⅔ cups medium-
    dry (hard) cider
   1 large or 2 small onions
   about 30 whole cloves
   3 bay leaves
   10 black peppercorns
   45ml/3 tbsp soft light brown sugar
   bunch of flat leaf parsley, to garnish
For the cranberry sauce
   350g/12oz/3 cups cranberries
   175g/6oz/¾ cup soft light brown sugar
   grated rind and juice of
    2 clementines
   30ml/2 tbsp port

1 Weigh the gammon and calculate the cooking time at 20 minutes per 450g/1lb, then place it in a large flameproof casserole or pan. Stud the onion or onions with 5–10 of the cloves and add to the casserole or pan with the bay leaves and peppercorns.

2 Add 1.2 litres/2 pints/5 cups of the cider and enough water just to cover the gammon. Heat until simmering and then carefully skim off the scum that rises to the surface using a large spoon or ladle. Start timing the cooking from the moment the stock begins to simmer.

3 Cover with a lid or foil and simmer gently for the calculated time. Towards the end of the cooking time, preheat the oven to 220°C/425°F/Gas 7.

4 Heat the sugar and remaining cider in a pan; stir until the sugar has dissolved.

5 Simmer for 5 minutes to make a dark, sticky glaze. Remove the pan from the heat and leave to cool for 5 minutes.

6 Lift the gammon out of the casserole or pan. Carefully and evenly, cut the rind from the meat, then score the fat into a diamond pattern. Place the gammon in a large roasting pan or ovenproof dish.

7 Press a clove into the centre of each diamond, then carefully spoon over the glaze. Bake for 20–25 minutes, or until the fat is brown, glistening and crisp.

8 To make the cranberry sauce, simmer all the ingredients in a heavy pan for 15–20 minutes, stirring frequently. Transfer the sauce to a jug (pitcher). Serve the gammon hot or cold, garnished with parsley and with the cranberry sauce.

COOK'S TIPS
• A large stockpot or preserving pan can be used in place of the casserole or pan for cooking the meat.
• Leave the gammon until it is just cool enough to handle before removing the rind. Snip off the string using a sharp knife or scissors, then carefully slice off the rind, leaving a thin, even layer of fat. Use a narrow-bladed, sharp knife for the best results.

VARIATION
Use honey in place of the soft brown sugar for the glaze and serve the meat with redcurrant sauce or jelly.

PAN-FRIED PORK WITH THYME AND GARLIC RISOTTO

LEAN PORK CHOPS ARE DELICIOUS SERVED WITH SMOOTH, CREAMY, BUT ROBUST RISOTTO IN THIS QUICK AND CONTEMPORARY MEAL.

3 To make the risotto, heat the butter with the oil in a large, heavy pan until foaming. Cook the shallots and garlic gently until the shallots are softened, but not coloured. Add the rice and thyme and stir until the grains are well coated with butter and oil.

4 Add a ladleful of boiling stock and cook gently, stirring occasionally. When all the stock is absorbed, add another ladleful. Continue cooking the risotto in this way until all the stock is absorbed. The secret of a good risotto is to have a pan of simmering stock ready and never to add too much at a time. The whole process should take 25–30 minutes. Season to taste.

SERVES FOUR

INGREDIENTS
    4 large pork chump or loin chops,
      each weighing about 175g/6oz,
      rind removed
    1 garlic clove, finely chopped
    juice of ½ lemon
    5ml/1 tsp soft light brown sugar
    25g/1oz/2 tbsp butter
    fresh thyme sprigs, to garnish
For the risotto
    25g/1oz/2 tbsp butter
    15ml/1 tbsp olive oil
    2 shallots, chopped
    2 garlic cloves, finely chopped
    250g/9oz/1⅓ cups risotto rice
    15ml/1 tbsp fresh thyme leaves
    900ml/1½ pints/3¾ cups boiling
      pork or chicken stock
    salt and ground black pepper

1 Put the chops in a shallow dish, and sprinkle the garlic over. To make the marinade, mix the lemon juice and soft light brown sugar together, and drizzle this over the chops.

2 Turn the chops to coat both sides with the lemon mixture, then cover the dish and leave the chops to marinate in the refrigerator while making the risotto.

5 Cook the chops when the risotto is half cooked. Melt the butter in a large, heavy frying pan. Remove the chops from the marinade, allowing the lemon juice to drip off, and fry them for 3–4 minutes on each side.

6 Divide the risotto among 4 plates and arrange the chops on top. Serve at once, garnished with fresh thyme.

MINI PORK AND BACON PIES

THESE LITTLE PIES CAN BE MADE UP TO A DAY AHEAD OF BEING SERVED AND THEY ARE A GOOD CHOICE FOR A SUMMER PICNIC OR SPECIAL PACKED LUNCH.

MAKES TWELVE

INGREDIENTS
10ml/2 tsp sunflower oil
1 onion, chopped
225g/8oz pork, coarsely chopped
115g/4oz cooked bacon, finely diced
45ml/3 tbsp chopped mixed fresh
  herbs, such as sage, parsley
  and oregano
6 eggs, hard-boiled (hard-cooked)
  and halved
1 egg yolk, beaten
20g/¾oz packet powdered aspic
300ml/½ pint/1¼ cups boiling water
salt and ground black pepper
For the pastry
450g/1lb/4 cups plain
  (all-purpose) flour
115g/4oz/½ cup white vegetable fat
  or lard (shortening)
275ml/9fl oz/generous 1 cup water

1 To make the pastry, sift the flour into a bowl and add a pinch of salt and pepper. Gently heat the fat and water in a large pan until the fat has melted. Increase the heat and bring to the boil.

2 Remove the pan from the heat and pour the liquid into the flour, stirring. Using the back of a spoon, press the mixture into a smooth ball of dough. Cover the bowl and set it aside. Preheat the oven to 200°C/400°F/Gas 6.

3 Heat the oil in a frying pan, add the onion and cook until soft. Stir in the pork and bacon and cook until browning. Remove from the heat and stir in the herbs and seasoning.

4 Roll out two-thirds of the pastry on a lightly floured work surface. Use a 12cm/4½in round cutter to stamp out rounds to line 12 muffin tins (pans). Place a little meat mixture in each pie, then add half an egg to each and top with the remaining meat.

5 Roll out the remaining pastry and use a 7.5cm/3in round cutter to stamp out lids for the pies. Dampen the rims of the pastry bases and press the lids in place. Pinch the edges to seal. Brush with egg yolk and make a small hole in the top of each pie to allow the steam to escape. Bake for 30–35 minutes. Leave to cool for 15 minutes, then transfer to a wire rack to cool completely.

6 Meanwhile, stir the aspic powder into the boiling water until dissolved. Shape a piece of foil into a little funnel and use this to guide a little aspic in through the hole in the top of each pie. Leave them to cool and set, then chill for up to 24 hours before serving.

STIR-FRIED PORK WITH MUSHROOMS

PORK TENDERLOIN IS THE PERFECT CUT FOR STIR-FRYING — IT IS LEAN AND COOKS IN MINUTES WHEN CUT INTO FINE STRIPS.

SERVES FOUR

INGREDIENTS
30ml/2 tbsp sesame oil
450g/1lb pork tenderloin, cut into
  fine strips
1 onion, halved and sliced
1 green chilli, seeded and
  roughly chopped
2 garlic cloves, sliced
150g/5oz oyster mushrooms, sliced
200g/7oz green beans, sliced
2 oranges, peeled and cut
  into segments
15ml/1 tbsp clear honey
30ml/2 tbsp sherry
To serve
350g/12oz egg noodles, cooked
30ml/2 tbsp sesame oil

1 Heat the sesame oil in a wok or large frying pan until very hot (almost smoking). Stir-fry the pork in three batches for 2 minutes each, or until crisp. Remove each batch in turn, then add the onion, chilli, garlic, oyster mushrooms and beans. Stir-fry the vegetables for 3–5 minutes.

2 Return the pork to the wok. Add the orange segments, honey and sherry, and cook for a further 2 minutes, stirring frequently.

COOK'S TIP
When stir-frying, cut the ingredients into similar size strips so that they cook evenly and quickly, and prepare all the ingredients before you begin cooking.

3 Prepare the egg noodles in a separate pan or wok. Heat the oil and stir-fry the cooked noodles for 2–3 minutes, or until hot, then divide them among warm serving bowls and spoon the pork stir-fry on top. Serve immediately.

SWEET-AND-SOUR RIBS OF PORK WITH EGG-FRIED RICE

THIS IS AN ANGLO-AMERICAN TAKE ON CHINESE FOOD — HARDLY AUTHENTIC SICHUAN BUT TERRIFICALLY TASTY NONETHELESS.

SERVES FOUR

INGREDIENTS
2 shallots, chopped
1 garlic clove, chopped
30ml/2 tbsp tomato purée (paste)
45ml/3 tbsp orange marmalade
30ml/2 tbsp light soy sauce
grated rind and juice of 1 orange
grated rind and juice of 1 lemon
1.5kg/3¼lb meaty pork ribs
salt and ground black pepper
For the egg-fried rice
30ml/2 tbsp sunflower oil
6 spring onions (scallions), sliced
1 red (bell) pepper, seeded
  and chopped
175g/6oz/1½ cups peas
2 eggs, lightly beaten
350g/12oz/1⅔ cups long grain
  rice, cooked

1 Preheat the oven to 200°C/400°F/ Gas 6. Mix the shallots, garlic, tomato purée, marmalade, soy sauce, orange and lemon rind and juice in a pan. Bring to the boil, stirring, then simmer until reduced to a syrupy glaze. Season with salt and pepper.

2 Arrange the pork ribs in a roasting pan. Drizzle the glaze over the ribs and bake for 30–40 minutes, turning occasionally and basting with the glaze.

3 Meanwhile prepare the egg-fried rice. Heat the oil in a large frying pan and cook the spring onions, pepper and peas until just tender. Add the lightly beaten eggs and cook until they are just beginning to set, then beat vigorously. Add the cooked rice and cook, stirring often, until piping hot.

4 Serve the rice on individual warmed plates, topped with the well-browned and glazed pork ribs.

NOISETTES OF PORK WITH CREAMY CALVADOS AND APPLE SAUCE

THIS DISH GIVES THE IMPRESSION OF BEING FAR MORE DIFFICULT TO PREPARE THAN IT REALLY IS, SO IT IS IDEAL AS PART OF A FORMAL MENU TO IMPRESS GUESTS. BUTTERED GNOCCHI OR GRIDDLED POLENTA AND RED CABBAGE ARE SUITABLE ACCOMPANIMENTS.

SERVES FOUR

INGREDIENTS

30ml/2 tbsp plain (all-purpose) flour
4 x 175g/6oz noisettes of pork
25g/1oz/2 tbsp butter
4 baby leeks, finely sliced
5ml/1 tsp mustard seeds,
  coarsely crushed
30ml/2 tbsp Calvados
150ml/¼ pint/⅔ cup dry white wine
2 eating apples, peeled, cored
  and sliced
150ml/¼ pint/⅔ cup double
  (heavy) cream
30ml/2 tbsp chopped fresh parsley
salt and ground black pepper

1 Place the flour in a bowl and add plenty of seasoning. Turn the noisettes in the flour mixture to coat them lightly.

2 Melt the butter in a heavy frying pan and cook the noisettes until golden on both sides. Remove from the pan and set aside.

3 Add the leeks to the fat remaining in the pan and cook for 5 minutes. Stir in the mustard seeds and pour in the Calvados, then carefully ignite it to burn off the alcohol. When the flames have died down pour in the wine and replace the pork. Cook gently for 10 minutes, turning the pork frequently.

4 Add the sliced apples and cream and simmer for 5 minutes, or until the apples are tender and the sauce is thick, rich and creamy. Taste for seasoning, then stir in the chopped parsley and serve immediately.

PORK AND BACON RILLETTES WITH ONION SALAD

RILLETTES IS POTTED MEAT, THE MOST FAMOUS OF WHICH IS MADE IN TOURS, FRANCE FROM PORK AND HAM. THIS VERSION MAKES A GREAT FIRST COURSE, DELICIOUS SNACK OR LIGHT MEAL.

SERVES EIGHT

INGREDIENTS

1.8kg/4lb belly (side) of pork, boned and diced, bones reserved
450g/1lb rindless streaky (fatty) bacon, finely chopped
5ml/1 tsp salt
1.5ml/¼ tsp freshly ground black pepper
4 garlic cloves, finely chopped
2 fresh parsley sprigs
1 bay leaf
2 fresh thyme sprigs
1 fresh sage sprig
300ml/½ pint/1¼ cups water
crusty French bread, to serve
For the onion salad
1 small red onion, halved and finely sliced
2 spring onions (scallions), cut into matchstick strips
2 celery sticks, cut into matchstick strips
15ml/1 tbsp freshly squeezed lemon juice
15ml/1 tbsp light olive oil
ground black pepper

1 In a large bowl, mix the pork, bacon and salt. Cover and leave at room temperature for 30 minutes. Preheat the oven to 150°C/300°F/Gas 2. Stir the pepper and garlic into the meat. Tie the herbs together to make a bouquet garni and mix this into the meat.

2 Spread the meat mixture in a large roasting pan and pour in the water. Place the bones on top and cover tightly with foil. Cook for 3½ hours.

3 Discard the bones and herbs, and ladle the meat mixture into a metal strainer set over a large bowl. Allow the liquid to drain through into the bowl, then turn the meat into a shallow dish. Repeat until all the meat is drained. Reserve the liquid. Use 2 forks to pull the meat apart into fine shreds.

4 Line a 1.5 litre/2½ pint/6¼ cup terrine or deep, straight-sided dish with clear film (plastic wrap) and spoon the shredded meat into it. Strain the reserved liquid through a sieve lined with muslin (cheesecloth) and pour it over the meat. Leave to cool. Cover and chill in the refrigerator for at least 24 hours, or until the rillettes has set.

COOK'S TIP
Ask the butcher to bone and chop the pork and to let you have the bones because they add flavour to the rillettes.

5 To make the onion salad, place the sliced onion, spring onions and celery in a bowl. Add the lemon juice and light olive oil and toss gently. Season with a little freshly ground black pepper, but do not add any salt as the rillettes is well salted.

6 Serve the rillettes, cut into thick slices, on individual plates with a little onion salad and thick slices of French bread and unsalted (sweet) butter.

FETTUCCINE WITH HAM AND PEAS

THIS SIMPLE DISH MAKES A VERY GOOD FIRST COURSE FOR SIX PEOPLE, OR A MAIN COURSE FOR THREE TO FOUR. THE INGREDIENTS ARE ALL READILY AVAILABLE FROM THE SUPERMARKET, SO THE RECIPE MAKES AN IDEAL IMPROMPTU SUPPER.

SERVES THREE TO SIX

INGREDIENTS
50g/2oz/¼ cup butter
1 small onion, finely chopped
200g/7oz/1¾ cups fresh or
    frozen peas
100ml/3½fl oz/scant ½ cup
    chicken stock
2.5ml/½ tsp granulated sugar
175ml/6fl oz/¾ cup dry white wine
350g/12oz fresh fettucine
75g/3oz piece cooked ham, cut into
    bitesize chunks
115g/4oz/1⅓ cups freshly grated
    Parmesan cheese
salt and ground black pepper

1 Melt the butter in a medium skillet or pan, add the onion and cook over a low heat for about 5 minutes until softened but not coloured.

2 Add the peas, stock and sugar, with salt and pepper to taste.

3 Bring to the boil, then lower the heat and simmer for 3–5 minutes or until the peas are tender. Add the white wine, increase the heat and boil until the wine has reduced.

4 Cook the pasta according to the instructions on the packet.

5 When the pasta is almost *al dente*, add the cooked ham to the sauce, with about one-third of the grated Parmesan. Heat through, stirring, then taste for seasoning. Adjust if necessary.

6 Drain the pasta and tip it into a warmed large bowl. Pour the sauce over and toss well. Serve immediately, sprinkled with the remaining grated Parmesan cheese.

CARBONARA ABRUZZI

IN ITALY, A DISH SERVED ALLA CARBONARA COMES WITH A SAUCE MADE FROM EGGS, OLIVE OIL, CREAM AND STRIPS OF BACON. THE NAME IS TAKEN FROM A NINETEENTH-CENTURY SECRET SOCIETY, THE PURPOSE OF WHICH WAS TO ACHIEVE A UNITED ITALY, WITH MEMBERS DISGUISED AS CHARCOAL BURNERS — CARBONARI — WORKING IN THE FOREST OF ABRUZZI.

SERVES FOUR

INGREDIENTS

500g/1¼lb spaghetti
30ml/2 tbsp olive oil
450g/1lb unsmoked back (lean)
  bacon, cut into strips
1–2 garlic cloves, finely chopped
2 eggs, beaten
300ml/½ pint/1¼ cups single
  (light) cream
25g/1oz Parmesan cheese, coarsely
  grated, plus extra for serving
30ml/2 tbsp chopped fresh parsley
salt and ground black pepper

COOK'S TIP

This dish cools very quickly, so warm the serving bowls in advance and serve the pasta immediately it is cooked. It also overcooks easily, so, if you have guests, make sure that they are seated and ready to eat before you add the egg mixture.

1 Cook the spaghetti in a very large pan of boiling salted water for about 10 minutes, or according to the packet instructions, until *al dente*: tender but with a bit of bite.

2 Meanwhile, heat the oil in a large, heavy frying pan (it must be large enough to hold the cooked spaghetti). Cook the bacon and garlic for about 10 minutes, stirring frequently, or until the bacon is golden. Drain the spaghetti.

3 Beat the eggs, cream, Parmesan and pepper. Add the hot spaghetti to the bacon and mix well. Pour in the egg mixture and cook for about 1 minute, turning the spaghetti all the time using tongs or a spoon and fork. Do not overcook the mixture or the eggs and cream will curdle.

4 Serve at once, spooned into warmed, shallow bowls and scattered with a little Parmesan and chopped parsley.

STUFFED PORK THAI OMELETTES

THAI FOOD OFTEN CLEVERLY COMBINES SAVOURY AND SWEET FLAVOURS, AS IN THE FILLING FOR THESE OMELETTES. IT MAKES AN INTERESTING CONTRAST TO THE STRONGER FLAVOUR OF THE PORK.

SERVES FOUR

INGREDIENTS
30ml/2 tbsp vegetable oil
2 garlic cloves, finely chopped
225g/8oz/2 cups minced
   (ground) pork
30ml/2 tbsp Thai fish sauce
5ml/1 tsp granulated sugar
2 tomatoes, peeled and chopped
15ml/1 tsp chopped fresh
   coriander (cilantro)
ground black pepper
sprigs of coriander and red chillies,
   sliced, to garnish
For the omelettes
5–6 eggs
15ml/1 tbsp Thai fish sauce
30ml/2 tbsp vegetable oil

1 Heat the oil in a wok, add the garlic, and fry for 3–4 minutes until soft. Add the pork and fry for about 8 minutes until lightly browned.

2 Stir in the fish sauce, sugar, tomatoes and pepper to taste; simmer until slightly thickened. Mix in the coriander.

3 To make the omelettes, whisk together the eggs and fish sauce.

4 Heat 15ml/1 tbsp of the oil in an omelette pan or wok. Add half the beaten egg mixture and tilt the pan to spread the egg into a thin, even layer.

5 Cook until the omelette is just set, then spoon half the filling into the centre. Fold into a neat square parcel by bringing the opposite sides of the omelette towards each other – first the top and bottom, then the right and left sides.

6 Slide the parcel on to a warm serving dish, folded side down. Repeat with the rest of the oil, eggs and filling to make a second omelette parcel. Garnish with sprigs of coriander and red chillies. Cut each omelette in half to serve.

COOK'S TIP
For a milder flavour, discard the seeds and membrane of the chillies where most of their heat resides. Always remember to wash your hands immediately after handling chillies, or wear gloves.

MUFFINS WITH BACON, EGGS AND QUICK HOLLANDAISE SAUCE

THIS MAKES A TERRIFIC CELEBRATION BREAKFAST, IDEAL FOR BIRTHDAYS, ANNIVERSARIES OR OTHER DAYS WHEN YOU WANT TO SET OUT WITH A SMILE ON YOUR FACE. YOU WILL NEED A BLENDER OR FOOD PROCESSOR TO MAKE THE SPEEDY VERSION OF HOLLANDAISE SAUCE.

2 Fill a large frying pan with water and bring to the boil. Add the vinegar and regulate the heat so that the water simmers. Crack the eggs into the water and poach them for 3–4 minutes, or slightly longer for firm eggs.

3 Split and toast the muffins while the eggs are cooking. Spread with butter and place on warmed plates.

4 To make the hollandaise sauce, process the egg yolks and white wine vinegar in a blender or food processor. Melt the butter. With the motor still running, very gradually add the hot melted butter through the feeder tube. The hot butter will cook the yolks to make a thick, glossy sauce. Switch off the machine as soon as all the butter has been added and the sauce has thickened. Season to taste.

5 Arrange the bacon on the muffins and add a poached egg to each. Top with a spoonful of sauce and grind over some black pepper. Serve immediately.

SERVES FOUR

INGREDIENTS
  350g/12oz rindless back (lean) bacon rashers (strips)
  dash of white wine vinegar
  4 eggs
  4 English muffins
  butter, for spreading
  salt and ground black pepper
For the hollandaise sauce
  2 egg yolks
  5ml/1 tsp white wine vinegar
  75g/3oz/6 tbsp butter

1 Preheat the grill (broiler) and cook the bacon for 5–8 minutes, turning once, or until crisp and brown on both sides.

COOK'S TIPS
Eggs that are a week or more old will not keep their shape when poached so, for the best results, use very fresh free-range organic eggs. To make sure that you don't break the yolk, crack the eggs into a cup before carefully adding them to the gently simmering water.

SAUSAGE, CURED MEAT AND OFFAL DISHES

Richly flavoured, and extremely good to eat, sausages and offal (innards) are used to create some of the tastiest dishes in the world. Cassoulet de Languedoc and Devilled Kidneys are classic dishes, but this chapter also includes modern meal ideas, such as Crunchy Salad with Black Pudding. Cured meats can be used as the main ingredient, or combined with other meats as a flavour enhancer. The recipes in this chapter are light and modern, easy to shop for and quick to prepare and cook. There are wonderfully warm salads, tasty appetizers, speedy snacks and stunning dinner-party dishes.

MEDITERRANEAN SAUSAGE AND PESTO SOUP

THIS HEARTY SOUP MAKES A SATISFYING ONE-POT MEAL THAT BRINGS THE SUMMERY FLAVOUR OF BASIL TO MIDWINTER MEALS. THICK SLICES OF WARM CRUSTY BREAD MAKE THE PERFECT ACCOMPANIMENT.

SERVES FOUR

INGREDIENTS
  15ml/1 tbsp olive oil, plus extra
    for frying
  1 red onion, chopped
  450g/1lb smoked pork sausages
  225g/8oz/1 cup red lentils
  400g/14oz can chopped tomatoes
  1 litre/1¾ pints/4 cups water
  oil, for deep-frying
  salt and ground black pepper
  60ml/4 tbsp pesto and fresh basil
    sprigs, to garnish

1 Heat the oil in a large pan and cook the onion until softened. Coarsely chop all the sausages except 1 and add them to the pan. Cook for about 5 minutes, stirring, or until the sausages are cooked.

2 Stir in the lentils, tomatoes and water, and bring to the boil. Reduce the heat, cover and simmer for about 20 minutes. Cool the soup slightly before puréeing it in a blender. Return the soup to the rinsed-out pan.

3 Cook the remaining sausage in a little oil in a small frying pan for 10 minutes, turning it often, or until lightly browned and firm. Transfer to a chopping board or plate and leave to cool slightly, then slice thinly.

4 Heat the oil for deep-frying to 190°C/375°F or until a cube of day-old bread browns in about 60 seconds. Deep-fry the sausage slices and basil briefly until the sausages are brown and the basil leaves are crisp.

5 Lift them out using a slotted spoon and drain on kitchen paper.

6 Reheat the soup, add seasoning to taste, then ladle into warmed individual soup bowls. Sprinkle with the deep-fried sausage slices and basil and swirl a little pesto through each portion. Serve with warm crusty bread.

ITALIAN SAUSAGES WITH PANCETTA AND BEANS

VARIATIONS ON THE THEME OF SAUSAGE AND BEAN STEW ARE FOUND IN MOST COUNTRIES AS AN INEXPENSIVE, EASY AND HEARTY PEASANT DISH. BAKED POTATOES OR CREAMY MASHED POTATOES ARE AN EXCELLENT ACCOMPANIMENT FOR THE STEW.

SERVES FOUR

INGREDIENTS
15ml/1 tbsp sunflower oil
12 Italian spicy fresh pork sausages
50g/2oz pancetta, chopped
2 onions, quartered
2 garlic cloves, crushed
1 red (bell) pepper, halved, seeded
   and sliced
2 x 400g/14oz cans chopped
   tomatoes
400g/14oz can cannellini beans,
   drained and rinsed
salt and ground black pepper

VARIATION
Use beef or lamb sausages in place of the pork sausages, substitute chopped leeks for the onions and add a finely chopped and seeded red chilli along with the pepper. Serve with polenta.

1 Pour the sunflower oil into a flameproof casserole and add the sausages and pancetta. Cook over a medium heat for about 10 minutes, turning the sausages and pancetta occasionally, or until the pancetta is crispy and the sausages are golden brown. Be careful to moderate the heat – if it is too fierce the sausages will burst. Use a draining spoon to remove the sausages and pancetta from the casserole and set aside.

2 Discard any excess fat and add the onions and garlic. Cook for about 5 minutes over a high heat, stirring frequently. Add the pepper and cook for about 2–3 minutes.

3 Replace the sausages and pancetta and stir in the tomatoes and beans. Heat until simmering, then cover and simmer for about 20 minutes, stirring occasionally. Season to taste.

CASSOULET DE LANGUEDOC

THERE ARE MANY REGIONAL VARIATIONS OF THIS CLASSIC FRENCH CASSEROLE OF SAUSAGE, BEANS AND ASSORTED MEATS, EACH WIDELY DIFFERENT FROM THE NEXT ACCORDING TO ITS TOWN OF ORIGIN. IN LANGUEDOC ALONE, THE TOWNS OF TOULOUSE, CASTELNAUDARY AND CARCASSONNE ALL CLAIM TO BE THE HISTORICAL HOME OF THE AUTHENTIC CASSOULET.

SERVES EIGHT

INGREDIENTS

225g/8oz/1¼ cups dried haricot
    (navy) beans, soaked for 24 hours
2 large onions, 1 cut into chunks
    and 1 chopped
1 large carrot, quartered
2 cloves
small handful of parsley stalks
225g/8oz lean gammon (cured ham),
    in one piece
4 duck leg quarters, split into thighs
    and drumsticks
225g/8oz lean lamb, trimmed and cubed
2 garlic cloves, finely chopped
75ml/5 tbsp dry white wine
175g/6oz cooked Toulouse sausage,
    or garlic sausage, skinned and
    coarsely chopped
400g/14oz can chopped tomatoes
salt and ground black pepper
For the topping
    75g/3oz/1½ cups fresh white
        breadcrumbs
    30ml/2 tbsp chopped fresh parsley
    2 garlic cloves, finely chopped

1 Drain and rinse the beans, then place them in a large pan and add the onion chunks, carrot, cloves and parsley stalks. Pour in enough cold water to cover and bring to the boil.

2 Boil the beans for 10 minutes, then reduce the heat, cover and simmer for 1½ hours, or until the beans are tender. Skim off any scum that rises to the surface and top up with boiling water as necessary. Drain the cooked beans, reserving the stock; discard the onion, carrot, cloves and parsley stalks.

3 Put the gammon into a pan and cover with cold water. Bring to the boil, reduce the heat and simmer for 10 minutes. Drain and discard the water, leave until cool enough to handle, then cut the meat into chunks. Preheat the oven to 150°C/300°F/Gas 2.

4 Heat a large, flameproof casserole and cook the duck portions in batches until golden brown on all sides. Use a draining spoon to remove the duck portions from the casserole, set aside. Add and brown the trimmed and cubed lamb in batches, removing each batch and setting aside.

5 Pour off the excess fat from the casserole, leaving about 30ml/2 tbsp. Cook the chopped onion and garlic in this fat until softened. Stir in the wine and remove from the heat.

6 Spoon a layer of beans into the casserole. Add the duck, then the lamb, gammon, sausage, tomatoes and more beans. Season each layer. Pour in enough of the reserved stock to cover the ingredients. Cover, and cook in the oven for 2½ hours. Check occasionally to ensure the beans are covered, add more stock if necessary.

7 Mix together the topping ingredients and sprinkle over the cassoulet. Cook, uncovered, for a further 30 minutes.

PORK AND LEEK SAUSAGES WITH MUSTARD MASHED POTATO AND ONION GRAVY

LONG, SLOW COOKING IS THE TRICK TO REMEMBER FOR GOOD ONION GRAVY AS THIS REDUCES AND CARAMELIZES THE ONIONS TO CREATE A WONDERFULLY SWEET FLAVOUR. DO NOT BE ALARMED AT THE NUMBER OF ONIONS — THEY REDUCE DRAMATICALLY IN VOLUME DURING COOKING.

SERVES FOUR

INGREDIENTS
 12 pork and leek sausages
For the onion gravy
 30ml/2 tbsp olive oil
 25g/1oz/2 tbsp butter
 8 onions, sliced
 5ml/1 tsp caster (superfine) sugar
 15ml/1 tbsp plain (all-purpose) flour
 300ml/½ pint/1¼ cups beef stock
For the mashed potato
 1.5kg/3¼lb potatoes
 50g/2oz/¼ cup butter
 150ml/¼ pint/⅔ cup double
  (heavy) cream
 15ml/1 tbsp wholegrain mustard

1 To make the onion gravy, heat the oil and butter in a large pan until foaming. Add the onions slices and mix well to thoroughly coat them in the fat. Cover and cook gently for about 30 minutes, stirring frequently. Add the sugar and cook for a further 5 minutes, or until the onions are softened, reduced and slightly caramelized.

2 Remove the pan from the heat and stir in the flour, then gradually stir in the stock. Return the pan to the heat. Bring to the boil, stirring, then simmer for 3 minutes, or until thickened. Season.

VARIATION
For pesto mashed potato, omit the mustard and add 15ml/1 tbsp pesto, 2 crushed garlic cloves and olive oil.

3 Meanwhile, cook the potatoes and the pork and leek sausages. First, cook the potatoes in a pan of boiling salted water for 20 minutes, or until tender.

4 Drain the potatoes well and mash them well with the butter, cream and wholegrain mustard. Season with salt and pepper to taste.

5 While the potatoes are cooking, preheat the grill (broiler) to medium. Arrange the sausages in a single layer in the grill pan and cook for 15–20 minutes, or until cooked, turning frequently so that they brown evenly.

6 Serve the sausages with the creamy mashed potato and onion gravy.

VENISON SAUSAGES WITH RED WINE GRAVY AND POLENTA

STRONGLY FLAVOURED, MEATY SAUSAGES ARE DELICIOUS WITH ROBUST RED WINE AND ASSERTIVE SHIITAKE MUSHROOMS. SERVE WITH PLENTY OF POLENTA TO MOP UP THE DELICIOUS GRAVY.

3 Sprinkle in the flour and gradually pour in the wine, stirring and pushing the sausages around to mix the flour and liquid smoothly with the leeks.

4 Bring slowly to the boil, reduce the heat and simmer for 10–15 minutes, stirring occasionally, or until the wine sauce is smooth and glossy.

SERVES FOUR

INGREDIENTS
    15ml/1 tbsp sunflower oil (optional)
    12 venison or wild boar sausages
    2 leeks, sliced
    2 plump cloves garlic, sliced
    225g/8oz/3¼ cups shiitake
      mushrooms, quartered
    15ml/1 tbsp plain (all-purpose) flour
    600ml/1 pint/2½ cups red wine
    30ml/2 tbsp chopped mixed fresh
      herbs, such as flat leaf parsley
      and marjoram
    salt and ground black pepper
For the polenta
    750ml/1¼ pints/3 cups water
    175g/6oz/1½ cups instant polenta
    50g/2oz/¼ cup butter

1 Pour the oil, if using, into a large frying pan, add the sausages and cook over a medium heat for 15–20 minutes, turning frequently.

2 Add the leeks, garlic and mushrooms and mix well. Cook the vegetables for 10–15 minutes, or until the leeks are soft and beginning to brown.

5 Meanwhile, cook the instant polenta. Pour the water into a pan and add a little salt, then bring it to the boil. Sprinkle in the polenta, stirring constantly, and cook for 4–5 minutes, stirring constantly, or until thick and smooth. Remove the pan from the heat, beat in the butter and season to taste with salt and pepper.

6 Season the red wine sauce with salt and pepper to taste and sprinkle the herbs over the sausages. To serve, put a large ladleful of polenta into each serving dish or deep plate (soup plates or pasta dishes are ideal) and top with the sausages, leeks and sauce.

DUCK SAUSAGES WITH SPICY PLUM SAUCE

RICH DUCK SAUSAGES ARE BEST BAKED IN THEIR OWN JUICES RATHER THAN FLASHED UNDER THE GRILL. CREAMY MASHED SWEET POTATOES AND SPICY PLUM SAUCE COMPLEMENT AND CONTRAST WITH THE RICHNESS OF THE SAUSAGES.

SERVES FOUR

INGREDIENTS

8–12 duck sausages
1.5kg/3¼lb sweet potatoes, cut
  into chunks
25g/1oz/2 tbsp butter
60ml/4 tbsp milk
salt and ground black pepper
For the plum sauce
30ml/2 tbsp olive oil
1 small onion, chopped
1 small red chilli, seeded and
  finely chopped
450g/1lb plums, stoned (pitted)
  and chopped
30ml/2 tbsp red wine vinegar
45ml/3 tbsp clear honey

1 Preheat the oven to 190°C/375°F/ Gas 5. Arrange the duck sausages in a single layer in a large, shallow ovenproof dish and bake, uncovered, for about 25–30 minutes, turning the sausages 2–3 times during cooking, to ensure that they brown and cook evenly.

2 Meanwhile, put the sweet potatoes in a pan and pour in enough water to cover them. Bring to the boil, reduce the heat and simmer for 20 minutes, or until tender. Drain and mash the potatoes, then place the pan over a low heat. Stir frequently for about 5 minutes to dry out the mashed potato. Beat in the butter and milk, season.

3 Heat the oil in a small pan and fry the onion and chilli gently for 5 minutes. Stir in the plums, vinegar and honey, then simmer gently for 10 minutes.

4 Serve the freshly cooked sausages with the sweet potato mash and piquant plum sauce.

CHUNKY SAUSAGE ROLLS

OLD-FASHIONED SAUSAGE ROLLS, MADE WITH GOOD-QUALITY MEAT, HAVE A FABULOUS FLAVOUR WHICH THEIR BOUGHT ALTERNATIVES CANNOT MATCH.

MAKES TWELVE

INGREDIENTS
225g/8oz/2 cups plain
(all-purpose) flour
2.5ml/½ tsp English (hot)
mustard powder
115g/4oz/½ cup butter
15g/½oz Parmesan cheese,
finely grated
40ml/8 tsp iced water
450g/1lb good-quality sausagemeat
(bulk sausage)
5ml/1 tsp chilli sauce or garlic sauce
beaten egg, to glaze

1 Preheat the oven to 190°C/375°F/
Gas 5. Sift the flour and mustard into a
bowl. Rub in the butter until the mixture
resembles fine crumbs and stir in the
cheese. Mix in enough iced water to
make a soft dough. Wrap the dough in
clear film (plastic wrap) and chill.

2 Mix the sausagemeat with the chilli
sauce or garlic sauce and divide it into
12 equal portions. Use your hands to
shape each portion into a sausage
measuring about 7.5cm/3in long.

VARIATION
To make cocktail sausage rolls, cut each
large roll into 4 equal small slices, making
48 in total. Bake the mini sausage
rolls at 190°C/375°F/Gas 5 for about
10 minutes, or until cooked through.

3 Roll out the pastry to a 20 x 45cm/
8 x 18in rectangle and cut into
12 equal rectangles. Place a sausage in
the middle of each, brush the edges of
the pastry with water and roll it over the
sausage to enclose it completely. Place
on a baking sheet with the joins
underneath. Chill for 10 minutes. Brush
the sausage rolls with beaten egg and
bake for 20 minutes, or until golden
and cooked. Serve the sausage rolls
warm or cold.

TOAD-IN-THE-HOLE

THIS IS ONE OF THOSE DISHES THAT IS CLASSIC COMFORT FOOD – REMEMBERED AS A CHILDHOOD FAVOURITE AND PERFECT FOR LIFTING THE SPIRITS ON COLD DAYS. USE ONLY THE BEST SAUSAGES.

SERVES FOUR TO SIX

INGREDIENTS
175g/6oz/1½ cups plain (all-
purpose) flour
30ml/2 tbsp chopped fresh chives
2 eggs
300ml/½ pint/1¼ cups milk
50g/2oz/¼ cup white vegetable
fat or lard (shortening)
450g/1lb Cumberland sausages or
good-quality pork sausages
salt and ground black pepper

VARIATION
For a young children's supper, omit the
chives and cook cocktail sausages in
patty tins (muffin pans) until golden.
Add the batter and cook for 10–15
minutes, until puffed and golden.

1 Preheat the oven to 220°C/425°F/
Gas 7. Sift the flour into a bowl with a
pinch of salt and pepper. Make a well
in the centre of the flour. Whisk the
chives with the eggs and milk, then
pour this into the well in the flour.
Gradually whisk the flour into the liquid
to make a smooth batter. Cover and
leave to stand for at least 30 minutes.

2 Put the fat into a roasting pan and
place in the oven for 3–5 minutes. Add
the sausages and cook for 15 minutes.
Turn the sausages twice during cooking.

3 Pour the batter over the sausages
and return to the oven. Cook for about
20 minutes, or until the batter is risen
and golden. Serve immediately.

PAN-FRIED CALF'S LIVER
WITH CRISP ONIONS

SAUTÉED OR CREAMY MASHED POTATOES GO WELL WITH FRIED CALF'S LIVER. SERVE A SALAD OF MIXED LEAVES WITH PLENTY OF DELICATE FRESH HERBS, SUCH AS FENNEL, DILL AND PARSLEY, TO COMPLEMENT THE SIMPLE FLAVOURS OF THIS MAIN COURSE.

SERVES FOUR

INGREDIENTS
50g/2oz/¼ cup butter
4 onions, finely sliced
5ml/1 tsp caster (superfine) sugar
4 slices calf's liver, each weighing
  about 115g/4oz
30ml/2 tbsp plain (all-purpose) flour
30ml/2 tbsp olive oil
salt and ground black pepper
fresh parsley, to garnish

1 Melt the butter in a large, heavy pan with a lid. Add the onions and mix well to coat with butter. Cover the pan with a tight-fitting lid and cook gently for 10 minutes, stirring occasionally.

2 Stir in the sugar and cover the pan. Cook the onions for 10 minutes more, or until they are soft and golden. Increase the heat, remove the lid and stir the onions over a high heat until they are deep gold and crisp. Use a slotted spoon to remove the onions from the pan, draining off the fat.

3 Meanwhile, rinse the calf's liver in cold water and pat it dry on kitchen paper. Season the flour, put it on a plate and turn the slices of liver in it until they are lightly coated in flour.

COOK'S TIP
Take care not to cook the liver for too long as this may cause it to toughen.

4 Heat the oil in a large frying pan, add the liver and cook for about 2 minutes on each side, or until lightly browned and just firm. Arrange the liver on warmed plates, with the crisp onions. Garnish with parsley and serve with sautéed or mashed potatoes.

LAMB'S LIVER AND BACON CASSEROLE

BOILED NEW POTATOES TOSSED IN LOTS OF BUTTER GO WELL WITH THIS SIMPLE CASSEROLE. THE TRICK WHEN COOKING LIVER IS TO SEAL IT QUICKLY, THEN SIMMER IT GENTLY AND BRIEFLY. PROLONGED AND/OR FIERCE COOKING MAKES LIVER HARD AND GRAINY.

SERVES FOUR

INGREDIENTS
    30ml/2 tbsp sunflower oil
    225g/8oz rindless unsmoked back
        (lean) bacon rashers (strips)
    2 onions, halved and sliced
    175g/6oz/2⅓ cups chestnut
        mushrooms or button (white)
        mushrooms, halved
    450g/1lb lamb's liver, trimmed
        and sliced
    25g/1oz/2 tbsp butter
    15ml/1 tbsp soy sauce
    30ml/2 tbsp plain (all-purpose) flour
    150ml/¼ pint/⅔ cup chicken stock
    salt and ground black pepper

1 Heat the oil in a frying pan. Chop the bacon and fry until crisp. Add the onions to the pan and cook for about 10 minutes, stirring frequently, or until softened. Add the mushrooms to the pan and fry for a further 1 minute.

2 Use a slotted spoon to remove the bacon and vegetables from the pan and set aside. Add the liver to the pan and cook over a high heat for 3–4 minutes, turning once to seal the slices on both sides. Remove the liver from the pan and keep warm.

3 Melt the butter in the pan, add the soy sauce and flour and blend together. Stir in the stock and bring to the boil, stirring until thickened. Return the liver and vegetables to the pan and heat through for 1 minute. Season with salt and pepper to taste, and serve at once with new potatoes and lightly cooked green beans.

CRUNCHY SALAD <u>WITH</u> BLACK PUDDING

BLACK PUDDING IS A TYPE OF SAUSAGE ENRICHED WITH BLOOD AND FLAVOURED WITH SPICES. IN BRITAIN, IT IS THOUGHT OF AS A LANCASHIRE SPECIALITY, BUT SIMILAR SAUSAGES ARE ALSO FOUND ALL OVER EUROPE. FRIED UNTIL CRISP, SLICES OF BLACK PUDDING ARE EXTREMELY GOOD IN SALAD, PARTICULARLY WITH CRUNCHY BREAD CROÛTONS AND SWEET CHERRY TOMATOES. SERVE THIS SALAD IN BOWLS OR SHALLOW SOUP PLATES.

SERVES FOUR

INGREDIENTS
    250g/9oz black pudding (blood
      sausage), sliced
    1 focaccia loaf, plain or flavoured
      with sun-dried tomatoes, garlic
      and herbs, cut into chunks
    45ml/3 tbsp olive oil
    1 cos (romaine) lettuce, torn into
      bitesize pieces
    250g/9oz cherry tomatoes, halved
For the dressing
    juice of 1 lemon
    90ml/6 tbsp olive oil
    10ml/2 tsp French mustard
    15ml/1 tbsp clear honey
    30ml/2 tbsp chopped fresh herbs,
      such as coriander (cilantro), chives
      and parsley
    salt and ground black pepper

1 Dry-fry the black pudding in a large, non-stick frying pan for 5–10 minutes, or until browned and crisp, turning occasionally. Remove the black pudding from the pan using a slotted spoon and drain thoroughly on kitchen paper. Set the black pudding aside on a plate and keep warm.

VARIATION
If you are unsure of black pudding, then try this recipe with spicy chorizo or Kabanos sausages instead. Cut them into thick diagonal slices before cooking. Use another crusty bread, such as ciabatta for the croûtons, if you prefer.

2 While the black pudding is cooking, cut the focaccia into chunks. Add the oil to the juices in the frying pan and cook the focaccia cubes in two batches, turning often, until golden on all sides. Drain the focaccia on kitchen paper.

3 Mix together the focaccia, black pudding, lettuce and cherry tomatoes in a large bowl. Mix together the dressing ingredients and season with salt and pepper. Pour the dressing over the salad. Mix well and serve at once.

DEVILLED KIDNEYS ON BRIOCHE CROÛTES

THE EXPRESSION "DEVILLED" DATES FROM THE 18TH CENTURY. IT WAS USED TO DESCRIBE DISHES OR FOODS THAT WERE SEASONED WITH HOT SPICES, GIVING A FIERY FLAVOUR THAT WAS ASSOCIATED WITH THE DEVIL AND THE HEAT OF HELL.

SERVES FOUR

INGREDIENTS
8 mini brioche slices
25g/1oz/2 tbsp butter
1 shallot, finely chopped
2 garlic cloves, finely chopped
115g/4oz/1½ cups mushrooms
1.5ml/¼ tsp cayenne pepper
15ml/1 tbsp Worcestershire sauce
8 lamb's kidneys, halved and trimmed
150ml/¼ pint/⅔ cup double (heavy) cream
30ml/2 tbsp chopped fresh parsley

1 Preheat the grill (broiler) and toast the brioche slices until golden brown on both sides. Remove and keep warm.

2 Melt the butter in the pan until it is foaming. Halve the mushrooms and add to the pan with the shallot and garlic, then cook for 5 minutes. Stir in the cayenne pepper and Worcestershire sauce and simmer for about 1 minute.

3 Add the kidneys to the pan and cook for 3–5 minutes on each side. Finally, stir in the cream and simmer for about 2 minutes, or until the sauce is heated through and slightly thickened.

4 Remove the brioche croûtes from the wire rack and place on warmed plates. Top with the kidneys. Sprinkle with chopped parsley and serve immediately.

COOK'S TIPS
If you can't find mini brioches, you can use a large brioche instead. Slice it thickly and stamp out croûtes using a 5cm/2in round cutter. If you prefer, the brioche croûtes can be fried rather than toasted. Melt 25g/1oz/2 tbsp butter in a frying pan and fry the croûtes until golden. Remove from the pan and drain on kitchen paper.

CHICKEN LIVER PÂTÉ

THIS IS ONE OF THE SIMPLEST PÂTÉS TO MAKE AND IT TASTES EXCELLENT WITH CRISP MELBA TOAST.

SERVES FOUR

INGREDIENTS
    115g/4oz/½ cup butter
    4 shallots, finely chopped
    2 garlic cloves, finely chopped
    225g/8oz chicken livers, rinsed
        and trimmed
    30ml/2 tbsp dry sherry
    300ml/½ pint/1¼ cups double
        (heavy) cream
    salt and ground black pepper
To garnish
    mixed fresh herbs
    lemon or orange slices

COOK'S TIP
Don't overcook the livers or they may
harden and become grainy in texture.
When cooked, they should be still very
slightly pink in the centre.

1 Melt half the butter in a large frying
pan. Add the shallots and garlic, and
cook until softened but not coloured.
Add the chicken livers and stir over a
medium heat for 8–10 minutes, or until
they are just firm and cooked through.

2 Purée the chicken liver mixture in a
blender with the remaining butter and
sherry, transfer to a bowl.

3 Lightly whip the cream until it stands
in soft peaks, then fold it into the
chicken liver mixture with seasoning to
taste. Spoon the pâté into a serving dish
and chill until set.

4 Serve spoonfuls of the pâté on large
plates, garnished with fresh herbs and
slices of lemon or orange. Serve with
Melba toast or warm crusty bread.

HAGGIS TARTLETS WITH BASHED NEEPS AND TATTIES

HAGGIS IS THE TRADITIONAL SCOTTISH SAUSAGE OF HIGHLY SPICED LAMB'S OFFAL BOUND WITH
OATMEAL, PACKED INTO A LAMB'S STOMACH READY FOR GENTLE POACHING. THE CASING IS NOT EATEN,
BUT SPLIT OPEN SO THAT THE FILLING CAN BE SCOOPED OUT. THESE DAYS SYNTHETIC CASINGS ARE
USED AS WELL AS THE TRADITIONAL PAUNCH, BUT SINCE THIS IS NOT EATEN, IT DOES NOT MAKE ANY
DIFFERENCE OTHER THAN TO THE APPEARANCE.

SERVES EIGHT

INGREDIENTS
    450g/1lb haggis
    3 filo pastry sheets, each about 30 x
        20cm/12 x 8in, thawed if frozen
    25g/1oz/2 tbsp butter, melted
    90ml/6 tbsp whisky
    salt and ground black pepper
For the bashed neeps
    1 large swede (rutabaga), chopped
    45ml/3 tbsp double (heavy) cream
    50g/2oz/¼ cup butter
For the tatties
    900g/2lb potatoes, cut into chunks
    60ml/4 tbsp double (heavy) cream
    50g/2oz/¼ cup butter
    large pinch of grated nutmeg

1 Cook or reheat the haggis according
to the packet instructions. Preheat the
oven to 190°C/375°F/Gas 5.

2 Cut each sheet of filo pastry into 6
15cm/6in squares. Brush 8 sections of
a muffin tin (pan) with melted butter
and line each with a filo square. Brush
with butter and place a second piece of
pastry on top. Bake for 5–7 minutes, or
until crisp and pale golden.

3 Cook the swede and potato in
separate pans of boiling salted water for
20 minutes, until tender. Drain and
mash separately with cream and butter.
Season to taste and add a little nutmeg
to the potatoes.

4 Split the cooked haggis open and use
a teaspoon to scoop out the mixture,
dividing it among the filo tartlet cases.
Moisten each tartlet with a generous
amount of whisky and serve at once
with the bashed neeps and tatties.

PROSCIUTTO ᵂᴵᵀᴴ POTATO RÉMOULADE

RÉMOULADE IS A CLASSIC PIQUANT DRESSING BASED ON MAYONNAISE. THE TRADITIONAL FRENCH VERSION IS FLAVOURED WITH MUSTARD, GHERKINS, CAPERS AND HERBS, BUT SIMPLER VARIATIONS ARE SEASONED ONLY WITH MUSTARD. LIME JUICE BRINGS A CONTEMPORARY TWIST TO THIS RECIPE FOR A CREAM-ENRICHED DRESSING.

SERVES FOUR

INGREDIENTS

2 potatoes, each weighing about
  175g/6oz, quartered lengthways
150ml/¼ pint/⅔ cup mayonnaise
150ml/¼ pint/⅔ cup double
  (heavy) cream
5–10ml/1–2 tsp Dijon mustard
juice of ½ lime
30ml/2 tbsp olive oil
12 prosciutto slices
450g/1lb asparagus
  spears, halved
salt and ground black pepper
25g/1oz wild rocket, (arugula)
  to garnish
extra virgin olive oil, to serve

1 Put the potatoes in a pan. Add water to cover and bring to the boil. Add salt, then simmer for about 15 minutes, or until the potatoes are tender, but do not let them get too soft. Drain thoroughly and leave to cool and then cut into long, thin strips.

2 Beat together the mayonnaise, cream, mustard, lime juice and seasoning in a large bowl. Add the potatoes and stir carefully to coat them with the dressing.

3 Heat the oil in a griddle or frying pan and cook the prosciutto in batches until crisp and golden. Use a slotted spoon to remove the ham, draining each piece well. Cook the asparagus in the fat remaining in the pan for about 3 minutes, or until tender and golden.

4 Put a spoonful of potato rémoulade on each plate and top with several slices of prosciutto. Add the asparagus and garnish with rocket. Serve at once, offering olive oil to drizzle over.

CHICKEN BREASTS WITH SERRANO HAM

THIS MODERN SPANISH DISH IS LIGHT AND VERY EASY TO MAKE. IT LOOKS FABULOUS, TOO.

SERVES FOUR

INGREDIENTS

4 skinless, boneless
  chicken breast portions
4 slices Serrano ham
75g/3oz/6 tbsp butter
30ml/2 tbsp chopped capers
30ml/2 tbsp fresh thyme leaves
1 large lemon, cut lengthways
  into 8 slices
a few small fresh thyme sprigs
salt and ground black pepper

COOK'S TIP
This dish is just as good with other thinly
sliced cured ham, such as prosciutto, in
place of the Serrano ham.

1 Preheat the oven to 200°C/400°F/
Gas 6. Wrap each chicken breast
portion loosely in clear film (plastic
wrap) and beat with a rolling pin until
slightly flattened. Arrange the chicken
in a large, shallow ovenproof dish, then
top each with a slice of Serrano ham.

2 Beat the butter with the capers,
thyme and seasoning until well mixed.
Divide the butter into quarters and
shape each into a neat portion, then
place on each ham-topped chicken
portion. Arrange 2 lemon slices on the
butter and sprinkle with small thyme
sprigs. Bake for 25 minutes, or until
the chicken is cooked through.

3 To serve, transfer the chicken
portions to a warmed serving platter or
individual plates and spoon the piquant,
buttery juices over the top. Serve at
once, with boiled new potatoes and
steamed broccoli or mangetouts (snow
peas). Discard the lemon slices before
serving, if you prefer.

PROSCIUTTO AND MOZZARELLA PARCELS ON FRISÉE SALAD

PROSCIUTTO IS ITALIAN FOR HAM, PROBABLY THE MOST FAMOUS OF WHICH (TO NON-ITALIANS) IS PARMA HAM. THE NAME IS A VARIATION ON PRESCIUTTO WHICH MEANS, LITERALLY, DRIED BEFOREHAND. THE TYPES OF PROSCIUTTO VARY ACCORDING TO THE PARTICULAR CURING PROCESS USED.

SERVES SIX

INGREDIENTS
a little hot chilli sauce
6 prosciutto crudo slices
200g/7oz mozzarella, cut into 6 slices
6 filo pastry sheets, each measuring
   45 x 28cm/18 x 11in, thawed
   if frozen
50g/2oz/¼ cup butter, melted
150g/5oz frisée lettuce, to serve

COOK'S TIP
Prosciutto di Parma is readily available, usually along with at least one other type of prosciutto, but visit a good Italian delicatessen and you will find a choice of regional hams.

1 Preheat the oven to 200°C/400°F/ Gas 6. Sprinkle a little of the chilli sauce over each slice of prosciutto crudo. Place a slice of mozzarella on each piece of ham, then fold the ham around the cheese to enclose the slices of cheese completely.

2 Brush a sheet of filo pastry with a little melted butter and fold it in half to give a double-thick piece measuring 23 x 14cm/9 x 5½in. Place a ham and mozzarella parcel on the middle of the pastry and brush the remaining pastry with a little butter, then fold it over to enclose the ham and mozzarella in a neat parcel. Place on a baking sheet with the edges of the pastry underneath and brush with a little butter. Repeat with the remaining parcels and pastry sheets.

3 Bake the filo parcels for 15 minutes, or until the pastry is crisp and evenly golden. Arrange the lettuce on 6 plates and add the parcels. Serve at once.

SMOKED CHICKEN WITH PEACH MAYONNAISE IN FILO TARTLETS

THESE ARE ATTRACTIVE AND, BECAUSE SMOKED CHICKEN IS SOLD READY COOKED, THEY REQUIRE THE MINIMUM OF CULINARY EFFORT. THE FILLING CAN BE PREPARED A DAY IN ADVANCE AND CHILLED, BUT DO NOT FILL THE PASTRY CASES UNTIL YOU ARE READY TO SERVE THEM OR THEY WILL BECOME SOGGY.

MAKES TWELVE

INGREDIENTS
25g/1oz/2 tbsp butter
3 sheets filo pastry, each measuring
   45 x 28cm /18 x 11in, thawed
   if frozen
2 skinless, boneless smoked chicken
   breast portions, finely sliced
150ml/¼ pint/⅔ cup mayonnaise
grated rind of 1 lime
30ml/2 tbsp lime juice
2 ripe peaches, peeled, stoned
   (pitted) and chopped
salt and ground black pepper
fresh tarragon sprigs, lime slices and
   salad leaves, to garnish

1 Preheat the oven to 200°C/400°F/ Gas 6. Melt the butter in a small pan. Brush 12 small individual tartlet tins (muffin pans) with a little of the melted butter. Cut each sheet of filo pastry into 12 equal rounds large enough to line the tins, allowing enough to stand up above the tops.

2 Place a round of pastry in each tin and brush with a little butter, then add another round of pastry. Brush each with more butter and add a third round of pastry.

3 Bake the tartlets for 5 minutes, or until the pastry is golden brown. Leave in the tins for a few moments before transferring to a wire rack.

4 Mix the chicken, mayonnaise, lime rind and juice, peaches and seasoning. Chill this chicken mixture for at least 30 minutes, or up to 12 hours. When ready to serve, spoon the chicken mixture into the filo tartlets and garnish with tarragon sprigs, lime slices and salad leaves.

PASTA SALAD <u>WITH</u> SALAMI

THIS SALAD IS SIMPLE TO MAKE AND IT CAN BE PREPARED IN ADVANCE FOR A PERFECT APPETIZER OR, SERVED IN MORE GENEROUS QUANTITIES, TO MAKE A SATISFYING MAIN COURSE.

SERVES FOUR

INGREDIENTS

225g/8oz pasta twists
275g/10oz jar charcoal-roasted (bell) peppers in oil
115g/4oz/1 cup pitted black olives
4 sun-dried tomatoes, quartered
115g/4oz Roquefort cheese, crumbled
10 slices peppered salami, cut into strips
115g/4oz packet mixed leaf salad
30ml/2 tbsp white wine vinegar
30ml/2 tbsp chopped fresh oregano
2 garlic cloves, crushed
salt and ground black pepper

1 Cook the pasta in a large pan of boiling salted water for 12 minutes, or according to the instructions on the packet, until tender but not soft. Drain thoroughly and rinse with cold water, then drain again.

2 Drain the peppers and reserve 60ml/ 4 tbsp of the oil for the dressing. Cut the peppers into fine strips and mix them with the olives, sun-dried tomatoes and Roquefort in a large bowl. Stir in the pasta and peppered salami.

3 Divide the salad leaves among 4 individual bowls and spoon the pasta salad on top. Whisk the reserved oil with the wine vinegar, oregano, garlic and seasoning to taste. Spoon this dressing over the salad and serve at once.

VARIATION
Use chicken instead of the salami and cubes of Brie in place of the Roquefort.

WARM SALAD OF BAYONNE HAM AND NEW POTATOES

WITH A LIGHTLY SPICED NUTTY DRESSING, THIS WARM SALAD IS AS DELICIOUS AS IT IS FASHIONABLE, AND AN EXCELLENT CHOICE FOR INFORMAL ENTERTAINING.

SERVES FOUR

INGREDIENTS

225g/8oz new potatoes, halved
   if large
50g/2oz green beans
115g/4oz young spinach leaves
2 spring onions (scallions), sliced
4 eggs, hard-boiled (hard-cooked)
   and quartered
50g/2oz Bayonne ham, cut into strips
juice of ½ lemon
salt and ground black pepper
For the dressing
60ml/4 tbsp olive oil
5ml/1 tsp ground turmeric
5ml/1 tsp ground cumin
50g/2oz/⅓ cup shelled hazelnuts

1 Cook the potatoes in boiling salted water for 10–15 minutes, or until tender, then drain well. Cook the beans in boiling salted water for 2 minutes; drain.

2 Toss the potatoes and beans with the spinach and spring onions.

3 Arrange the hard-boiled egg quarters on the salad and arrange the strips of ham over the top. Sprinkle with the lemon juice and season with plenty of salt and pepper.

4 Heat the dressing ingredients in a large frying pan and continue to cook, stirring frequently, until the nuts turn golden. Pour the hot, nutty dressing over the salad and serve at once.

VARIATION
Replace the potatoes with a 400g/14oz can mixed beans and pulses. Drain and rinse the beans and pulses, then drain again. Toss lightly with the green beans and spring onions.

POTATO AND PEPPERONI TORTILLA

COOKED POTATOES ARE DELICIOUS WITH SPICY PEPPERONI IN A THICK SPANISH-STYLE OMELETTE.
SALAD AND CRUSTY BREAD ARE EXCELLENT ACCOMPANIMENTS.

SERVES FOUR

INGREDIENTS
    30ml/2 tbsp olive oil
    225g/8oz potatoes, cooked and cut
        into cubes
    75g/3oz pepperoni, sliced
    3 spring onions (scallions), sliced
    115g/4oz Fontina cheese, cut
        into cubes
    115g/4oz/1 cup frozen
        peas, thawed
    6 eggs
    30ml/2 tbsp chopped fresh parsley
    salt and ground black pepper

COOK'S TIP
If you do not have the confidence to
invert the tortilla and replace it in the
pan, simply finish cooking it under a
preheated grill (broiler) for 5–8 minutes.

1 Heat the oil in a non-stick frying pan
and add the potatoes, pepperoni and
spring onions. Cook over a high heat for
about 5 minutes, stirring. Stir in the
cheese and peas.

2 Beat the eggs with the parsley and
seasoning, then pour the mixture over
the ingredients in the frying pan. Cook
gently for about 10 minutes.

3 When the mixture has almost set,
cover the pan with a large plate and
carefully invert the pan and its cover to
turn out the tortilla. Slide the tortilla
back into the pan and continue cooking
for a further 10 minutes.

4 Turn out the tortilla on to a large, flat
platter and serve hot or warm, cut into
slices. Alternatively, leave until cold.

CHORIZO WITH GARLIC POTATOES

A CLASSIC TAPAS RECIPE, THIS SIMPLE DISH CAN BE SERVED IN SMALL QUANTITIES AS A SNACK OR,
AS HERE, IN SLIGHTLY LARGER PROPORTIONS FOR AN APPETIZER. THE NAME TAPAS IS DERIVED FROM
TAPA, A LID, TRADITIONALLY USED BY SPANISH BARMEN TO COVER GLASSES OF COLD FINO OR SHERRY
TO PREVENT FLIES FROM SETTLING IN THE DRINK. THE LID USUALLY TOOK THE FORM OF A SAUCER OF
SMALL CANAPÉS OR A SMALL PORTION OF A TASTY DISH TO BE ENJOYED WITH THE SHERRY.

SERVES FOUR

INGREDIENTS
    450g/1lb potatoes
    3 eggs, hard-boiled (hard-cooked)
        and quartered
    175g/6oz chorizo sausage, sliced
    150ml/¼ pint/⅔ cup mayonnaise
    150ml/¼ pint/⅔ cup sour cream
    2 garlic cloves, crushed
    salt and ground black pepper
    30ml/2 tbsp chopped fresh coriander
        (cilantro), to garnish

VARIATION
To give this dish a more piquant flavour,
add about 15ml/1 tbsp finely chopped
cornichons and 4 finely chopped canned
anchovy fillets.

1 Cook the potatoes in a pan of boiling
salted water for 20 minutes, or until
tender. Drain and leave to cool.

2 Cut the potatoes into bitesize pieces.
Place them in a large serving dish with
the eggs and chorizo sausage, and
season to taste with salt and pepper.

3 In a small bowl, stir the mayonnaise,
sour cream and garlic together with
seasoning to taste, then spoon this
dressing over the potato mixture.

4 Toss the salad gently to coat the
ingredients with dressing, then sprinkle
with chopped coriander.

BRESAOLA AND ROCKET PIZZA

ALTHOUGH THE ARMENIANS INITIATED THE IDEA OF TOPPING FLATTENED DOUGH WITH SAVOURY INGREDIENTS BEFORE BAKING IT, IT WAS THE ITALIANS – THE NEAPOLITANS IN PARTICULAR – WHO DEVELOPED THE PIZZA IN THE 1830s.

SERVES FOUR

INGREDIENTS
  150g/5oz packet pizza base mix
  120ml/4fl oz/½ cup lukewarm water
  225g/8oz/3¼ cups mixed
    wild mushrooms
  25g/1oz/2 tbsp butter
  2 garlic cloves, coarsely chopped
  60ml/4 tbsp pesto
  8 slices bresaola
  4 tomatoes, sliced
  75g/3oz/⅓ cup full-fat cream cheese
  25g/1oz rocket (arugula)

1 Preheat the oven to 200°C/400°F/Gas 6. Tip the packet of pizza base mix into a large mixing bowl and pour in enough of the water to mix to a soft, not sticky dough.

2 Turn out the dough on to a lightly floured surface and knead quickly and lightly for about 5 minutes, or until smooth and elastic. Divide the dough into 2 equal pieces, knead lightly to form 2 balls, then pat out the balls of dough into flat rounds.

3 Roll out each piece of dough on a lightly floured surface to a 23cm/9in round and transfer to baking sheets.

4 Slice the wild mushrooms. Melt the butter in a frying pan and cook the garlic for 2 minutes. Add the mushrooms and cook over a high heat for about 5 minutes, or until the mushrooms have softened but are not overcooked.

5 Spread pesto on the pizza bases, to within 2cm/¾in of the edge of each one. Arrange the bresaola and tomato slices around the rims of the pizzas, then spoon the cooked mushrooms into the middle.

6 Dot the cream cheese on top of the pizzas and bake for 15–18 minutes, or until the bases are crisp and the cheese just melted. Top each pizza with a handful of rocket leaves just before serving. Serve at once.

COOK'S TIP
If you are in a hurry, buy 2 ready-made pizza bases instead of the pizza mix and bake for 10 minutes.

ROASTED VEGETABLE <u>AND</u> GARLIC SAUSAGE LOAF

STUFFED WITH CURED MEAT AND ROASTED VEGETABLES, THIS CRUSTY COB LOAF MAKES A COLOURFUL CENTREPIECE FOR A CASUAL SUMMER LUNCH. SERVE WITH FRESH GREEN SALAD LEAVES.

2 Put the peppers and leek in a roasting pan with the oil and cook for about 25 minutes, turning occasionally, or until the peppers have softened.

3 Spoon half of the pepper mixture into the loaf, pressing it down well with a spoon. Add the green beans, garlic sausage, eggs and cashew nuts, packing the layers down well. Season each layer before adding the next. Dot the soft cheese over the filling and top with the remaining peppers.

4 Replace the top of the loaf and bake it for 15–20 minutes, or until the filling is warmed through. Serve at once, cut into wedges or slices.

VARIATION
You can use a variety of different-shaped loaves, such as a large, uncut sandwich loaf, for this recipe. Hollow out the loaf and fill as above, then cut into slices.

COOK'S TIP
Don't throw away the soft centre of the loaf. It can be made into breadcrumbs and frozen for use in another recipe.

SERVES SIX

INGREDIENTS

1 large cob loaf
2 red (bell) peppers, quartered
 and seeded
1 large leek, sliced
90ml/6 tbsp olive oil
175g/6oz green beans, blanched
 and drained
75g/3oz garlic sausage
2 eggs, hard-boiled (hard-cooked)
 and quartered
115g/4oz/1 cup cashew nuts, toasted
75g/3oz/⅓ cup soft cheese with
 garlic and herbs
salt and ground black pepper

1 Preheat the oven to 220°C/425°F/ Gas 7. Slice the top off the loaf using a large serrated knife and set it aside, then cut out the soft centre, leaving the crust intact. Stand the crusty shell on a baking sheet.

SHOPPING INFORMATION

UNITED KINGDOM
Butchers' Shops
R. Allen and Co.
117 Mount Street
London W1Y 6HX
Tel: 020 7499 5831

A. Crombie and Son
97–101 Broughton Street
Edinburgh EH1 3RZ
Tel: 0131 556 7643

Harrods Food Hall
87 Brompton Road
London SW1X 7XL
Tel: 020 7730 1234

Harvey Nichols Food Hall
109–125 Knightsbridge
London SW1X 7RJ
Tel: 020 7235 5000

Ilford Kosher Meats
7 Beehive Lane
Ilford, Essex R61 3R6
Tel: 020 8554 3238

Jefferies
42 Coombe Road
Norbiton, Kingston
Surrey KT2 7AS
Tel: 020 8546 0453

Morawski (Polish delicatessen)
157 High Street
London NW10 4TR
Tel: 020 8965 5340

O'Hagan's Sausage Shop
Delling Lane
Bosham, Nr Chichester
PO18 8NN
Tel: 01243 574833

Randall & Aubin (specialize in
French cuts of meat)
14–16 Brewer Street
London W1R 3FS
Tel: 020 7287 4447

SW7 Meat Emporium
19 Bute Street
London SW7 3EY
Tel: 020 7581 0210

Selfridges
400 Oxford Street
London W1A 1AB
Tel: 020 7629 1234

Simply Sausages
Hart's Corner
341 Central Markets
Farringdon Street
London EC1A 9NB
Tel: 020 7329 3227

Mail Order
Barrow Boar
Foster's Farm
South Barrow, Yeovil
Somerset BA22 7LN
Tel: 01963 440315
Fax: 01963 440901
Email: sales@barrowboar.co.uk

Donald Russell Direct
(traditionally reared meat)
Freepost SCO 4131
Harlaw Road
Inverurie
Aberdeenshire
AB51 4ZL
Tel: 01467 629666
Fax: 01467 629434

Cooking Equipment
Divertimenti
45–47 Wigmore Street
London W1H 9LA
Tel: 020 7935 0689
139 Fulham Road
London SW3 6SD
Tel: 020 7581 8065

Information Services
Meat and Livestock
Commission
Winterhill House
Snowdon Drive
Milton Keynes
Bucks MK6 1AX
Tel: 01908 677577
Fax: 01908 609826

AUSTRALIA
Meat & Livestock
Australia Limited
PO Box 4129
Sydney
NSW 2001
Tel: (02) 9463 9333
Fax: (02) 9463 9393

National Meat Association
Level 2
Albany Street
Crows Nest NSW 2060
Tel: (02) 9906 3769
Fax: (02) 9438 5144

UNITED STATES
Meat Suppliers
Albert's Prime Meats
836 Lexington Avenue
New York, NY 10021
Tel: (212) 751 3169
Web site:
www.albertandsons.com

American Beefalo
International
P.O. Box 656
Somerset, KY 42502
Tel: (800) BEEFALO
www.ababeefalo.org

Virginia's Buffalo Meats, Inc.
P.O. Box 456
Blue Ridge, VA 24064
Tel: (54) 977 5976
www.vbmeats.com

Cooking Equipment
Bowery Kitchen Supply
The Chelsea Market
460 West 16th Street
New York, NY 10011
Tel: (212) 376 4982
www.bowerykitchens.com

Chef's Catalog
P.O. Box 620048
Dallas, TX 75262 0048
Tel: (800) 884-CHEF
www.chefscatalog.com

Information Services
U.S. Department of
Agriculture
14th & Independence Ave. SW
Washington, D.C. 20250
Tel: (202) 720 2791
www.usda.gov

North American Deer Farmers
Association
9301 Annapolis Road 206
Lanham, MD 20706 3115
Tel: (301) 459 7708
Fax: (301) 459 7864
www.nadefa.org

BIBLIOGRAPHY

The Book Of Ingredients by Philip Dowell and Adrian Bailey (Mermaid, 1983)

A Concise Encyclopedia Of Gastronomy by André L Simon (Penguin, 1983)

Le Cordon Bleu Techniques & Recipes: Meat by Jeni Wright and Eric Treuille (Cassell, 1998)

The Diner's Dictionary by John Ayto (Oxford University Press, 1993)

English Food by Jane Grigson (Penguin, 1993)

Food by Clarissa Dickson Wright (Ebury, 1999)

The Food Chronology by James Trager (Aurum Press, 1996)

Food In England by Dorothy Hartley (Futura, 1985)

Fresh Ways With Beef & Veal (Time Life Books, 1986)

Fresh Ways With Lamb (Time Life Books, 1986)

Fresh Ways With Pork (Time Life Books, 1986)

The Good Housekeeping Cookery Book (Ebury Press, 1985)

A History Of Food by Maguelonne Toussaint-Samat (Blackwell, 1994)

How To Eat by Nigella Lawson (Chatto & Windus, 1998)

Larousse Gastronomique edited by Robert J. Coutine (Paul Hamlyn, 1988)

Ma Cuisine by Auguste Escoffier translated by Vyvyan Holland (Hamlyn, 1984)

Mastering The Art Of French Cooking by Simone Beck, Louisette Bertholle and Julia Child (Penguin, 1966)

Meat Course by Sophie Grigson (Network, 1995)

On Food And Cooking by Harold McGee (Allen & Unwin, 1986)

The Oxford Companion To Food by Alan Davidson (Oxford University Press, 1999)

Reader's Digest Complete Guide To Cookery by Anne Willan (Dorling Kindersley, 1989)

Le Répertoire de la Cuisine by Louis Saulnier (Leon Jaeggi, 1982)

The Rituals Of Dinner by Margaret Visser (Penguin, 1993)

Wine by Keith Richmond and Lucy Knox (Hamlyn, 1997)

The World Atlas Of Food edited by Jane Grigson (Mitchell Beazley, 1974)

ACKNOWLEDGEMENTS

Picture Acknowledgements

All photographs are by Craig Robertson and Janine Hosegood, except the following: Jon Whittaker pp130–31, 151; Sam Stowell p97; Cephas Picture Library p7t Hervé Champolion; Anthony Blake Photo Library p18t Jon Sims, p34t Keiran Scott, p44 Anthony Blake; Planet Earth Pictures p6b Geoff du Feu, p18b Brian Brown; BBC Natural History Unit p34b Davis Kjaer; Bruce Coleman Collection p6tr Mark N Boulton, p45 George McCarthy.

Publisher's Acknowledgements

The publishers would like to thank the following companies who supplied meat for photography: Keith Fisher of the Meat and Livestock Commission, and Fayre Game Ltd. We would also like to thank Magimix and Divertimenti for providing specialist cooking equipment for photography.

Authors' Acknowledgements

A book like this is an enormous undertaking and we could not have done it without the help and advice of a lot of people. We would like to thank Chris and Jeremy Godfrey who run the butcher's, Frank Godfrey Ltd in Islington, North London. We have learned a lot about meat by listening to them over the years. We also want to thank Keith Baker of the Meat and Livestock Commission, and Fred Mullion of the Worshipful Company of Butchers.

We want to thank Sarah Lowman for helping us test the recipes and Tina Fenner for keeping us organized; Joanna Farrow, Bridget Sargeson, Annabel Ford and Victoria Walters, the home economists who prepared the food for photography; Helen Trent, the stylist who found all the wonderful props; Craig Robertson and Janine Hosegood, who took the pictures; Bridget Jones and Susanna Tee, who edited the text; and Linda Fraser for offering us the project in the first place.

INDEX

NOTES

NOTES

NOTES

Notes

NOTES

NOTES

NOTES

NOTES

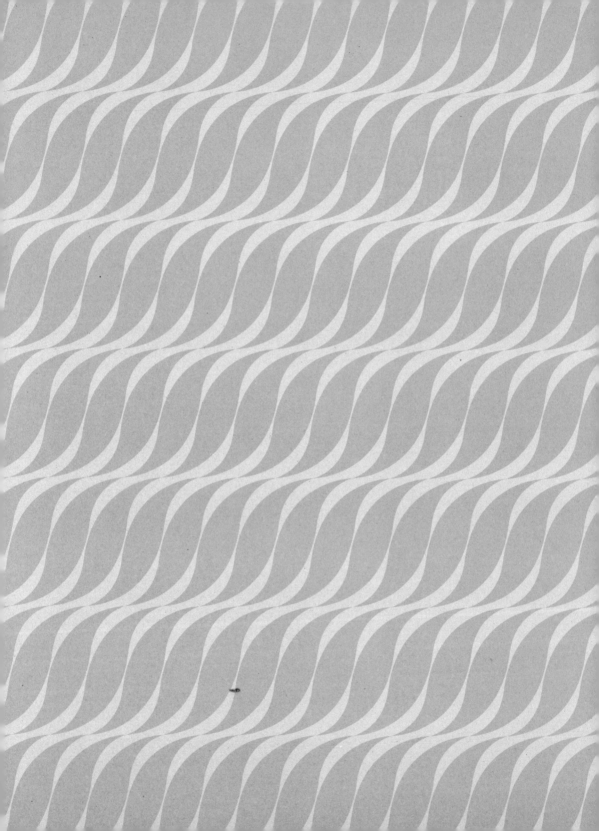